MW00774039

Dear Debbie

I am hugely gratified
for your interest in my book

With my very best wishes,

Theresa (Jerri)
Cerrigone
2013

I would love to hear from you!

# THE Silver Thread

## A MEMOIR

By

## THERESA CERRIGONE

PENTIMENTO PRESS

TRY TO REMEMBER (from "The Fantasticks")
Lyrics by TOM JONES
Music by HARVEY SCHMIDT
Copyright © 1960 (Renewed) by TOM JONES and HARVEY SCHMIDT
Publication and Allied Rights Assigned to CHAPPELL & CO., INC.
All Rights Reserved Used By Permission

Photographs from author's family collection
Edited by Carol Renzelman
Cover and book design by Tina Hedin

Printed in the United States of America
First Printing, 2013
ISBN: 978-0-9893997-0-8
Pentimento Press
115 Bradford Rd.
Keene NH 03431
pentimentopublishing.com

Dedicated to
The lights in my life:
Zack, Alyssa, Danielle, Luke, and Alexandra . . .
And especially to Christine and Claudine.

**Written in Loving Memory of my husband,
George.**

Heartfelt thanks
To the "Women of Memoir,"
Particularly Gladys Thompson Roth,
For her encouragement and inspiration.

Enormous appreciation to my editor,
Carol Renzelman,
Without whom this creation would have
Never found its way to print.

Thank you to Tina Hedin for cheering me on
And for her Artistry and Creative Talents.

~Theresa Cerrigone, 2013

# CONTENTS

## Acknowledgments

It is my pleasure to lovingly acknowledge
My parents, Rose and Rocco Giunta,
My brother, Bobby, my sister, Josephine,
and
My friend Connie Levin
For standing by my side,
And for being the very threads that have been
Woven together to create the colorful fabric of my
Memories

# Prologue

# This is My Story

MY HUSBAND, GEORGE, left our lives almost twenty years ago. A decade later I was compelled to chronicle the sad facts surrounding his devastating affliction. I began to write down the events that haunted me; the strange way George's story played out during the year he was gravely ill; the year he was attached by the silver thread.

I slept on George's side of the bed after he was gone, finding it surprisingly consoling. Sometimes leaping from under warm covers, I often rushed to the computer with a previously uncovered memory in my head. In the quiet darkness of the night, passages poured out, searching for the chalk-white page. The words that spilled over were comforting; they were telling the story of George. As I wrote, my remembrances took shape, the story grew, and other chapters of my life found their way onto the pages.

The original prologue morphed into several chapters about the astonishing tale of our baby girl, Claudine, and the life-threatening accident she suffered when she was just eighteen months old. Her dark days seemed oddly connected to George's.

As George and I travel those dark days, my story begins . . . and the narrative carries on with many silver threads unraveling and intertwining in my life.

Thus my memoir was born.

# 1

## Baby Claudine . . . 1971

PALE MORNING LIGHT stretched across the East River and filtered its way into the hospital window. It was Saturday morning at dawn. George stared sleepily at our tiny child lying motionless in the too-large crib. The room, so white, so plain and unadorned, appeared sterile. Eighteen-month-old Claudine wore only her diaper and a miniature blue hospital gown. Suddenly, the early morning stillness shattered as bright red blood escaped from our daughter's pink lips, staining the gown. Her dark eyes rolled back in her head. George, usually a quiet man, screamed for help. He looked on helplessly as nurses ran in; they had to stop the bleeding. The NYU Hospital team rushed about, a blur of white uniforms—powerfully efficient, transfusing that red life-supporting liquid into Claudine's little body, a body unable to live without it.

Our robust, curly-haired child had been admitted to NYU Hospital the previous day—my birthday—September 24, 1971, a sparkling fall Friday in our lively city.

Claudine had been sick on and off for two weeks. "She has an ear infection," one pediatrician said as he prescribed penicillin.

In our third floor walk-up, several weeks before Claudine's rush to the hospital in Manhattan, I had been alone with the baby and our four-year old daughter, Christine, when the unthinkable happened. Claudine convulsed as her eyelids fluttered. In seconds it had been over, except for the blood in her diaper. Frantic, I had called George. Soon we were attempting to navigate, as fast as possible, through congested streets to the hospital emergency room near our home. After they examined her, we had been sent away, doctors unalarmed: "Take her off the penicillin; it might be causing internal bleeding." One doctor on staff at the medical center where I routinely took the girls accused me of being a "hysterical mother" because I had called them daily about her fever, tummy pains, and bleeding. Another pediatrician asked, "Did you feed her red Jell-O?" Finally, after almost two weeks of anxiety, a voice of reason came from the baby's regular pediatrician, who had been away. She said, "Take Claudine to NYU Hospital for observation; we need to get to the bottom of this."

Looming before us, the angular modern hospital was uninviting, but it rested beside the East River just across from Long Island City where George and I had grown up. The river appeared calm and the Pepsi-Cola sign, a landmark of our childhood neighborhood, blinked comfortingly.

We were on the other side of the East River now—the Manhattan side. Those of us who lived in Queens, as we did—or in one of the other boroughs—ventured infrequently into Manhattan, except perhaps to go to work. When we did take the subway in, we said, "We're going to the City." Our side of the river was the other side—where our older sisters and brothers had jumped into the navy blue water on hot days, where, in back of the powerhouse, George had played football countless times with the guys until they were in their twenties. It was where we all had learned to drive, as there was little traffic. It was the side of the river where George's Italian family of three brothers and two sisters had grown up.

Maybe there were people here on the Manhattan side to help us. Perhaps we needn't be so frightened and shaky inside, because the best doctors were here at NYU Hospital. Now, after our frantic trips to the local hospital and numerous calls to the pediatrician—now, they would know I had been right. There was something wrong with our baby.

We dashed out of the car and into the hospital lobby to the reception desk, where the interrogation began. We answered questions; the baby was charming and endearing, fluctuating between dancing around and clutching her tummy. My heart almost broke while we answered their seemingly endless list of questions—I was consumed with the thought that Claudine might be getting sicker as we spoke. The attendant filled out pages of paperwork at the cold counter under harsh lights that hurt my already burning eyes.

Finally, Claudine was admitted to the pediatric ward. I thought I had heard them say she might be bleeding internally because her tiny fingernails seemed to be bloodless. She was isolated from other children in the unit because her condition was as yet undiagnosed and might be contagious, and George and I felt cut off from the rest of the hospital population. Minutes felt like hours, as we were intermittently left alone with the baby with no answers forthcoming.

For George and me, the strangeness of this place was striking—the sounds of babies crying alone in their cribs, or, just as distressing, staring at nothing and making no sounds at all. The odors of medicines and disinfectants invaded our nostrils. Who were all these people purposefully walking in and out, gleaning information from us, and pricking our little princess's fingers to find an answer in that tiny drop of blood? Always the waiting, answering the same questions each time a new staff person approached. We held our breath.

In between the questions, we cuddled and comforted our baby, and in that cuddling and comforting, her little fingers comforted us as she touched our faces and grasped our big fingers. Brightly colored puzzles amused her in the deserted nursery playroom, until staff hustled us out of there into a private room because she might be contagious. Fear hung in the air between George and me. We had been jarred from our neat little ordinary lives and nothing existed outside these unfamiliar walls.

Wearing his blue work shirt and pants and clunky black shoes, George looked out of place here, even to me. He was absent from his job as a tool and die maker at the factory, and me, my life as a stay-at-home mom was suspended. We were afraid, but truly didn't suspect how the next few days would unfold, each of us engrossed in our own uncertainties as we waited for the outcome, often looking into each other's faces, asking, "What is wrong with our baby?"

Claudie and Chrissi are little ones

I thought of our life just before our baby got sick: our cozy apartment and our little family—George and me, along with Claudine and our bright-eyed and lively little four-year-old daughter Christine—a family made complete by Sam and

7

June, our two rescued dogs. Now, Claudine would spend her first night in a strange hospital crib with George watching over her, while I waited at home with Christine, who knew nothing of the drama unfolding. Our firstborn daughter, Chrissi, with her great black eyes and George's shiny chestnut hair, was beloved by our family—her aunts and cousins doted on this young member of our nest of all-girl cousins. She was delighted to be able to spend the days with Aunt Jo and her cousins while George and I were preoccupied with her sick baby sister. Our plan was to take turns staying at the hospital at Claudine's bedside, so one of us could look after Chrissi at home in the evenings.

And then there were the dogs.

Years before, when a fluffy white ball of fur dashed across Queens Boulevard, a harrowing cross for people and animals alike, George had demanded I pull over so he could jump out of a still-moving automobile to grab the little dog, save it from certain death—or at least from being lost—and return it to its owner. This was just one instance that showed who George was when it came to animals. It was not surprising that during his routine of walking our own two dogs each night into the desolately quiet streets alongside the river and among the factories, he had established a ritual of feeding the strays. With Claudine hospitalized, we took turns taking care of our own dogs and feeding the strays as well.

The pediatric gastroenterologist on call that Saturday morning came to the hospital from his home in Westchester County. He may not have realized he was facing a long and difficult day in the operating room. George called me, his voice trembling, "Come to the hospital, right away." In my panic I could not drive, so our friend Charlie drove me to NYU Hospital. Charlie was a NYC police officer—it felt as if nothing could hurt me when I was with him. I remember the ride only as being silent and stifling—my shallow breathing the only sound.

George told me that as he had sipped a cup of strong coffee grabbed hurriedly from the cafeteria, he kept watch over Claudine. Then, "All hell broke loose," and the bleed had begun. What if he had still been in the cafeteria or in the elevator? What if he had not been there in the room with Claudine; would they have known she was hemorrhaging? She was hooked up to no machines, so nurses would not have been alerted to the calamity. What if she had still been at home, and had not already been admitted to the hospital? What had we miraculously averted? With that massive a hemorrhage, she would have been lost.

Time seemed to stand still as we heard the doctor say, "We have to go in to see what's going on." Our last glimpse of Claudine before surgery was in the elevator as she was rushed into the OR, blood-soaked towels wrapped around her little body. The elevator doors closed.

As we waited for word, George's face was contorted with anxiety. He stepped outside the hospital saying he "needed fresh air." Sitting on a hard wooden bench in the softly lit, candle-filled sanctuary of the nearby Catholic Church, George said his prayers and begged for his little girl to be safe.

We paced the spare halls and awaited news. "Will she be okay?" George and I pleaded as the youthful doctor walked toward us. He said, "She might have bleeding ulcers." *How could she have bleeding ulcers?* I thought. Repeating my mantra again after the dozens of times I had already spoken it to all who would listen, I said, "She puts everything in her mouth; couldn't she have swallowed something?"

George was inconsolable; he was scared. I, strangely calm, seemed to watch the scene from outside my body. I knew she would be saved; she had to be.

Oddly, I thought I might smoke a cigarette, although I had stopped smoking three years prior. *Smoking a cigarette is not going to help my child,* I reasoned. Family and friends came and went throughout the hazy day and night, trying their best to support us in our pain, saying all the words they thought we wanted to hear. We barely saw their faces or heard the whispers around us as we waited, one or the other of us constantly at Claudine's side.

# 2

# In the Beginning... 1955/1956

T HE UNIQUE FAIRYTALE love story that was George's and mine began fifteen years before Claudine got sick. It was not a simple story, nor would it ever be one.

"Can I wear a white dress to a New Year's Eve party?" I asked my older sister Josephine, as I pointed to a shiny white princess dress. "Of course," she said, "It's winter white." I tried on the pretty dress and it hugged my youthful curves. I was sixteen years old. The New Year's Eve party was to be my first date with George, and that dress marked the beginning of our love story.

George was twenty-one when we were introduced by our friend Mickey. The party was a family affair with our older brothers and sisters, along with neighborhood friends who joined the festivities at Muff's Boathouse in Queens. The Boathouse was a rustic, warm, and woody structure on the icy waters off La-Guardia Airport. I smile now as I think back on that evening. George was strikingly handsome in a dark suit. His eyes were so deeply brown they were nearly black and his olive skin appeared healthy and tan. He was always handsome, but then, so young, he was shy and so very appealing. He had not dated much, but I knew immediately he was smitten with me, gazing into my eyes and holding me close as we danced.

That night of the shimmering white dress was the beginning of romance for George and me. We went to the movies in the city the next day, New Year's Day. We held hands on the Number Seven train to Manhattan and again on the way home after sitting enraptured by the fabled story of Camelot.

In the months that followed, we went to movies at the Paramount or Radio City Music Hall, and concerts at Brooklyn Academy of Music. Together, we cheered at Boston Celtic and NY Knicks basketball games at Madison Square Garden—just some of the games feeding George's insatiable appetite for sports.

George and I had innocent fun when we were dating. We went out with friends from the old neighborhood, and went fishing on his little boat that had an outboard motor with a starting capacity that was always in doubt. We held hands and roamed Central Park during long afternoons and took trips on the ferry to Bear Mountain. George loved Broadway plays; he saw many of the great hits of the 50s and 60s, with now-legendary stars. Soon I was included in his sojourns into Manhattan theater life. *The Fantasticks,* a spectacular off-Broadway musical that ran for over forty years, was special for us. Our wedding song, "Try to Remember," was from that show. We ate scrumptious Italian delicacies at a tiny Italian restaurant

George—handsome always

called The Grotto. We always asked to be seated in the dark and sultry back room, where each table was dimly lit by a dripping candle in a Chianti bottle. There, the authentic grotto rocks lining the walls had a misty glow; we played at love amid the corny ambiance.

I was in high school and excited about my senior prom, startled when George called and said, "Well, I just got my draft notice and have to report before the prom." Tearfully, I soon said goodbye to my boyfriend.

George was sent to Fort Dix, New Jersey for basic training, and in a few months we were able to visit. As George's family and I headed for Jersey, I remembered that this was the second time I had visited the Army base at Fort Dix. My memory floated back to the time I was a little girl and my older brother Bob had been stationed there. My sister, Jo, seven years older than me, beautiful as always, had stood next to the piano in the recreation room with all the boys gaping at her glowing strawberry-blond hair and spectacular figure. I had been jealous, and I loved her, too.

When George was stationed at Fort Dix, his mother and the rest of her brood—with me in tow—had descended on the army base with macaroni and meatballs and other Italian treats for the dear boy before he traveled on. George and I continued our courtship long distance, as dozens of amorous letters crisscrossed the US to and from the bases where he served. I never went to the prom.

# 3

# Claudine and the Verdict ... 1971

HOURS LATER, ON THE DAY of the operation, the verdict was in. We listened with every nerve cell in our bodies. Dr. G. explained, "The baby swallowed a piece of a broom bristle and it acted like a needle, piercing her bowel early in the illness—thus the bloody diaper. It finally pierced a main artery leading from the aorta, causing the massive hemorrhage. We almost didn't find the piece of broom bristle, and were about to close, when we moved one of her tiny organs and saw the strange object."

We cried when we saw her in the ICU. Tubes were everywhere in her little body. The surgeon said, "Claudine is stable, but she won't be out of the woods for at least twenty-four hours. We'll be monitoring her vitals in the infant intensive care unit." The nurses and doctors regularly checked the warmth of her little left leg to be sure that the blood supply from the aorta was adequate.

Nurses dubbed our curly-haired cherubic baby "Claudine the Queen." She looked as though she were holding court, sitting up and looking around at everything and everyone, as her condition improved each passing day. She was not sick, as many of the babies on the ward were, so she looked chubby and healthy. When the "white coat people" came towards her, she cried out and clung to us, wanting only her precious binky to suck on. She was pricked and poked and frightened, and we cried again when we saw the pinpricks in all her fingers and toes because her blood was continually being scrutinized.

Throughout many of the seventeen days and especially the nights of her hospital stay, George was there watching over Claudine. On his "watch" he met and befriended another worried father sitting by his own son's bedside as the child recovered from open-heart surgery. They stood their vigils in the darkened rooms, and watched mice run from place to place. The hospital was under construction, and at night, the little creatures kept the whispering fathers company.

Our experience in that hospital haunted our dreams. After all, we were in the pediatric ward, where there were gravely ill children. Some of them had been there for months, and some would remain there until they died. Some died as we kept our vigil, and the hushed weeping was tragic. We could only turn away in horror. Some children had been there for long periods of time, and parents or caregivers sometimes came infrequently. We offered our help to those babies, feeding them or comforting them. The little boy whose mother had set her house on fire was horribly burned, scars disfiguring his face.

Many cradles held spina bifida babies, who would not survive. Sights and smells—especially the smells—were unforgettable, and those I would remember years into the future at George's desperate hospital bedside.

Hours ticked by, and then days blended in to one another. Mercifully, we were told that Claudine's little leg was safe, and in time all the tubes were removed. Our child survived and after all those days and nights, we joyfully took our baby home and resumed our life. We felt that our existence had changed forever.

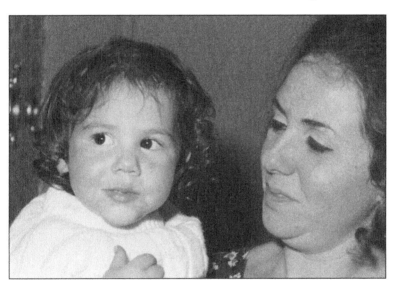

Mommy and Claudine, the day she came home from the hospital

Gratitude filled the months following our baby's operation. Claudine grew and thrived and only the bright red scar on her belly remained a constant reminder of the horror of our experience. Her accident had been remarkable—it was written up in the *Journal of the American Medical Association* for its unique significance.

# 4

# The Tragedy . . . 1992

WENTY-ONE YEARS SLIPPED peacefully by. George—my best friend and husband—and I were just beginning to revel in our almost-empty nest. Then, on another cool, bright and clear September morn that held no foreboding of the devastating day spreading out before us, George fell sick.

On September 14, 1992, the red message light on my office phone blinked incessantly and when I played the message, I heard George's voice, "Hi, it's me." I thought, *Oh, he must have called as usual to give me my laugh for the day, or to tell me he's crazy about me.* Minutes later the loud rings caught me again before I headed out to lunch. This time, his friend from work was on the line, saying, "George is very sick; he has chest pains, is nauseous, and he says the sunlight is stinging his eyes."

George and two friends from work had rushed to our home, where they were now frantically telephoning me. Though grateful for their care, I thought George might be having a heart attack, so I pleaded, "Take him to the nearby University Hospital—I'll meet you there."

The weather that day was glorious, but in my panic to meet George at the hospital, I hardly noticed. Feeling alone and vulnerable, my hands hurt from gripping the steering wheel as I drove. I wondered if I knew how to get to the hospital. I *had* to know, so I concentrated on the blacktop, following the white lines intently. I could not get lost.

Then the grey buildings loomed before me: *Which door should I enter? Where do I park?* I felt unglued.

Finding the emergency room, I was ushered to George's bedside. I hugged him and felt happy to see how handsome he looked. I had expected him to look sick, but he was just scared. So was I. I gazed around at the stark whiteness of the room as strangers appeared and disappeared. George said, "I don't belong here; I should be back at work." He saw the incredulity of it all.

In came the "green coats" and the "white coats," stethoscopes dangling. Each in turn placed their instruments against his heart; their faces gave no indication of what they heard. They asked the usual questions and took notes. Events began to unfold as in a surreal dream. I watched tearfully as tests seemed to be endlessly administered. I could barely keep track of the curious measures taking place before my eyes. I was certain something was terribly wrong. Was it a heart attack, or an episode even more sinister? As minutes turned into agonizing hours, the day moved both swiftly and slowly, until the golden

September day turned into a cool evening. Before any concrete answers came from medical staff, the sky was deep blue outside the hospital windows.

It was late, almost 9 p.m., when we were told, "We believe George has an ascending aortic aneurysm." I asked myself, *What is that?* He was wheeled away on a gurney to undergo an angiogram. Delicate surgery to repair his aorta was required, and soon the thoracic specialist, a young medical Fellow on staff, came in to talk to us, explaining the condition. I heard his words but they seemed unfamiliar as they bounced into the air. "George has an 85-to-90 percent chance of survival; he's young—only fifty-eight—healthy, and does not smoke." He confessed that this was a very serious surgery. My tears flowed, and I was admonished not to show them to George, as it might put him in distress. The doctor was reassuring as he made the fateful decision to postpone the operation until the morning, saying, "Tomorrow, there will be a full complement of staff available." Not realizing I should object or scream, "NO—do it now!" we remained silent. Afterward, when it was too late, the remorseful realization sank my heart: the operation should have been performed immediately, as it was so grave a condition that something could go dangerously wrong.

## George's Illness and Mistakes . . . 1992

A S DARKNESS SETTLED all around us in the tiny room, fate stepped in. I watched breathlessly as our daughters, Christine and Claudine, along with our future sons-in-law, Michael and Paul, rushed to the hospital to see George. Dear friends and family dropped everything to dash to his bedside that evening, though George had just been admitted. I was puzzled—friends and family usually visit *after* an operation. Something told them they had to come that night—that if they waited, it would be too late.

When George was transferred to a room in the cardiac area, he was in discomfort, but not in serious distress. In those few moments we had together that night, we were both terrified and feeling strangely isolated—as if we were the only two people in the world, enveloped in a now-starless night.

George seemed to be saying goodbye. He said, "No matter what happens, promise me that you will go on with the wedding." Our older daughter, Chrissi, was to be married in a few short weeks, and we were looking forward with great happiness to the joyous day. Dismissing his words, we refused to think of any such outcome. He said to our close next-door neighbors, John and Josephine, "I'm grateful for your friendship and to have you in our lives." John protested when he said that, and said, "I'll see you tomorrow."

That night, we held on to each other. "George is in good hands," we were told. The resident vowed she would "take good care of him." I trusted; why should I not trust? The doctor who first saw George in the emergency room was a young woman with whom Chrissi, our daughter, had attended college at Stony Brook. The last name of the resident in the cardiac care unit was the same as my mother's maiden name. Chrissi's good friend was on nursing duty, and she assured us she would look in on him. These were all good omens—or so we thought. Things were moving quickly; not much time to think, investigate, or seek information about how we should proceed, had this condition been known to us. I was asked to say good night and to come back in the morning. We kissed, and with apprehension, left the silent, sterile cocoon. It was near 11 p.m.

## A Timeless Connection

L ATER, ENGULFED IN YEARS of sadness, I pondered the month—September: the start of George's illness as well as the month of Claudine's accident; my birthday month and the month we began dating again after a break in our relationship; the month mentioned and highlighted in our wedding song. I looked back over my journals written during those years, and connections took shape. I remembered the days surrounding Claudine's operation and George's prayerful vigil. I found it strange and significant that his illness involved his aorta, the very same organ that had been pierced in our child's accident, and that month—September.

I have never been able to shake a gut feeling about my now-grown daughter Claudine, and her connection to George, along with the significance of September, that beautiful, terrible month.

I cannot help but wonder: did George plead with his God on that day in September—as he knelt on that unforgiving wooden kneeler—to save our child and take him instead? Did he make a promise to give his life if she were saved? George never alluded to having prayed in such a way, but a poem he wrote in 1971—one he had kept secret—affords a glimpse of his feelings surrounding our ordeal with Claudine. I found it among his things years later.

23

## For Claudine

When all seems dark and spirit's low,
Our daily grind that wears us so,

The daily tasks seem to bore us all,
The chores unending seem so tall.

As life is still and all is torn,
I still think of one September morn

When death was near and hope was nil,
A child was suffering a woeful ill.

There comes a time for very few
Who get to see what God can do.

When hope is thin, and gloom is near,
You pray your best to fight your fear.

The time goes slow with thoughts that chill,
You think the thoughts to help your will.

And young life is much in doubt,
And all your love seems to come right out.

It's years it seems for final word,
The dreaded sounds you wish unheard,

And you hear your child is well,
You finally emerge from a troubled hell.

And all the gold and worth can't buy,
You know your prize is love, you sigh!

# 5

# George's Early Days

B OTH IDYLLIC AND PAINFUL, I see George's childhood as flawed, as childhoods often are. Perhaps he might have gone to college, or been encouraged in sports. It was a different time and place, though.

He told me of precious memories playing the traditional street "stick ball" game with "the boys" in the shadow of the massive powerhouse in our little enclave of Long Island City. Now gentrified beyond our wildest dreams, luxury apartments with terraces take up every inch of space there and sumptuous lofts have been created where manufacturing used to take place. Across the river from Manhattan, it is a choice location.

When we were young and growing up in Long Island City, we marveled at the beautiful sights just down the block from our modest apartments. Gazing at the lighted, sparkling buildings

George—once more, so handsome

on warm summer evenings, we dreamed of that City, which might have been a backdrop for a spectacular movie. It was only later, after we were grown, that we realized how sublimely lucky we were to have lived in the shadow of our beloved city of lights.

To George, Long Island City was a fun place to live. He always had to be rounded up by one of his older brothers to come home for dinner. George's brother Dominic told me that he got many a whipping for not being able to drag his little brother home. The boys in the neighborhood were hesitant to rough up "Georgie," because the older Cerrigone boys would be after you if their little guy had been mistreated.

Dom told me that George was bad. He cursed when he was small, and everyone thought it was cute. It's funny, I never knew that about him: he was an imp, and misbehaved. I'm glad. It gives me a thrill to know he was devilish, because he often seemed too serious as an adult—except when he told his infamous jokes. Now I notice with pleasure his impish legacy in his grandchildren.

The youthful, carefree time was one that George recalled nostalgically. The neighborhood "boys" he played with became lifelong friends, and when they came together—even if years had elapsed—it was a special time. They talked about the old days, and reminisced about colorful neighborhood characters and the funny nicknames they were given: "Dudu," or "The Artist," or "Onions," or "The Greek." Over the years, there were picnics together, reunions, weddings, and sometimes, funerals. These friends conjure up memories of our courtship days and our youth.

One of the "boys" from the past wrote to me after George became sick. The letter was long and humorous and contained copies of other letters he had exchanged with George (the contents of which only those involved would understand). "We here have a wealth of great, humorous, and loving memories of 8th Street, and all 'the boys' who lived and played in L.I.C. Those who are not with us any longer are still here in our minds and hearts, and they still see us, watch over us, and love us more than we mortals ever can. When you speak to George, in the quiet of the night, ask him to get together with Tate, Vinny, Danny, and Mickey and 'pick a winner' [a stock for their venerable stock club] for 'the boys.'"

Until she died, George's mother lived in the home he had grown up in. It was the only apartment I ever visited and where the grandchildren gathered, almost weekly, for wonderful macaroni and braciole, and lasagna for holiday celebrations. Where my girls could go out a door in the

Terri as a little girl

kitchen to the blacktop-and-tar roof of the building next door, and pretend they were on a terrace. Where George had slept in a bedroom with two brothers, and where he departed to make a home with me on our wedding day. He saw the changes in his neighborhood, the people who moved away or died. But for me it remained a special neighborhood, where so many of the people were related or from the same town in Italy. It continues to be "the old neighborhood" for me, even with the vast changes over the years.

Family and friends visiting "the old neighborhood" sometimes to go to the New York City-style restaurants and try to recapture the safety and warmth of childhood. My youth was happily spent in Long Island City too, only a few short blocks away, near the courthouse and the "L" train. When I visit my block with the neat brownstones, they look so tiny; the elementary public school has the distinction of having been designated a landmark building, and is an experimental arts center. My sister and brother, and George and his brothers and sisters, attended PS#1. My mother had attended that school in the 1920s, and when I return with my grandchildren to show them where I spent my childhood, I am filled with pride and warmth.

During our marriage, I was sometimes frustrated that George was not more interested in reading. But over the years we were together, I glimpsed a contented man and recognized that this contentment was the success of his life. In our memory, we—his friends and family—recall him as having achieved that all-elusive happiness that the rest of us seem to be seeking. He cherished the simple things: among the best were spending time with his girls, watching sports on TV, being in his backyard with a dog or two at his side, and eating a good meal.

George loved baseball, and he was a poet.

He wrote this poem in 1947 at the tender age of thirteen:

## The Ending of the Ninth

The score was one to nothing, the ending of the ninth,
The pitcher was getting belted, then, taken out of sight.

The crowd arose, surprised to see . . .
The relieving pitcher, as calm as he could be,

He strode to the mound, with no fear at all,
And the first man went down, on a ground ball.

The visiting team stood up with a blow,
When the next man popped up to Phil Rizzuto,

The pinch hitter arose, surprised by all,
And went down on a tremendous fast ball,

He strode to the dugout, full of rage—
And among the men who hated Joe Page.

. . . And this one about football, when he was older:

## The Saga of Francis T.

When the year 2000 comes into view
There will be men to give those their due;
They will rank those who held some fame,

That got the headlines and also blame;
As they sort all those files,
Whose daily deeds we watched beguiled;
They will come to quarterbacks, who ruled so right,
The men who kept their team in the fight;

When all the data has been compiled,
The names will come forth of different styles.
They will talk of Sonny, Y.A., and "Slinging Sam,"
Of Bart N., Kemp, and that man Van;
And then come Parilli and Johnny U,
Followed by Blanda, Greese and Otto too;
And there'll be Brodie and Layne—that super foe,
Also Roger, Rote, and Broadway Joe;
They all performed to fans enthralled,
With feats of skill and of gone-by falls;

But as they read, they'll surely stop,
As a name appears that is near the top;
His stats are great, among the best,
In certain fields he leads the rest;
It's Francis T. of whom I speak,
His accomplishments acclaimed at his peak;

But they won't find any championship won,
When he was getting his job done;
And then they will say of Francis T.
A fair conclusion you'll surely see—

A super loser is best that can be said,
In second best of teams he led;

And as in sports only one can be proud,
And all the others are just faces in a crowd.

George wrote this poem many years ago in honor of a reunion to be held in the old neighborhood when we were young thirty-somethings.

It is winter dreariness throughout the land,
Bitter cold, to bear if you can,

Fortunate one am I to be
Through my eyes the future I see,

Rich men fly and poor men freeze,
With clothes they try the chill to ease.

I see brittle bones and frozen feet,
Animals in search of heat,

I see sickness, fever, colds, and the flu
They'll take their toll before they're through.

And all seems lost, that's all she wrote
But wait, I see a spark of hope.

On 30th March, the day I note
At Gigi's place I see merriment afloat.

And on that night at 9:00 p.m.,
I see old friends that meet again,

I see joy again come into sight
As pleasant happenings occur that night.

The Biped Club's 3rd Annual Blast
That makes the other two seem far in the past.

With food and drink for all to share,
Through music and dancing they forget their cares.

And all who come and get that glow
Will be carried through 'til melted snow

When birds with song and trees of green
Brighten our daily scene.

How lucky all.

# 6

## Dominic Shares Memories of George . . . 2013

A MAZINGLY, AT THE SWEET age of eighty-nine in this year 2013, George's older brother Dominic finally shared some of his memories of his little brother. This is what he told me:

"After eighty-nine years, you can imagine I have plenty of memories. Many of them are sometimes dim, but the memories of Georgie are as if they happened yesterday."

Dom confided, "Not a day goes by that I do not think of my little brother. When he was a kid I was responsible for him, being sent around the neighborhood to find him—God knows where!"

"Everybody in the neighborhood loved Georgie. 'Skipper'

Little George with brother Dom and sister Rose

became his nickname after one of the neighborhood gents promised to give him two cents if he would skip for him. He would skip, skip, and skip over and over again—each time getting just two cents. He was about five years old, and once when the guy teased Georgie and refused to give him the two cents, George called him a son-of-a-bitch."

"Aunt Jenny often took Georgie into her house to feed him and give him goodies. And when we couldn't find him, Aunt Jenny's would be the first place to look. Georgie loved their dog. They had a Chow Chow that once birthed twelve puppies. After frantically looking for him, I found him lying on the floor in their kitchen playing with the puppies, the mother dog close by. As I entered the kitchen, that mother dog took after me chasing me round and round the table, trying to bite me—but not George; he just blissfully played with the puppies."

"Aunt Jenny also had a nondescript black dog, and when she moved away with the dog and then came back after—oh, I would say eight or nine years, that black dog jumped up and hugged Georgie wildly, as if he had seen him yesterday."

"When I was in the Army, he sent me a poem . . . I don't remember the words, but the poem was something about the world . . . the war . . . Mussolini and Hitler—and that 'we won't be free until the boys come home.' I told my mom, 'That was a nice poem that Georgie's teacher wrote for the kids.' She wrote me back, 'The teacher didn't write that poem—Georgie did.' He was nine years old at the time."

"When we were older, I would come home from work late, and Georgie would be lying awake—at two or three o'clock in the morning: he would give me the baseball scores and tell me about all the great plays, sharing his enthusiasm for the game he was obsessed with."

As Dom and I talked about the old days, recalling moments from more than fifty years ago, my sister-in-law Ann (Dominic's wife) remembered, "We were at a party or dance in a big hall. Georgie, then in his twenties, saw that Theresa had arrived. He took off and jumped over tables and chairs across the room to get to her. I guess he was in love."

# 7

## Disaster . . . 1992

ALONE IN THE COZY, protected bedroom George and I shared, the shrill ring of the telephone frightened me to wakefulness. Barely asleep, I jumped to answer it. Fear struck my heart when I found that the hospital was calling me back in after having so recently sent me home to get some sleep. It was now 1:30 in the morning, and I could not believe this dreaded call was real.

On the line was the surgeon himself. He said, "The picture I painted earlier is not as rosy as I thought," and that "George's representatives should come to the hospital, as there has been an episode." I sensed tragedy. Without asking questions, we—my daughters and I—fairly flew back to the hospital. We drove through the darkened night on empty streets, unknowing and terrified as to what to expect. We raced through the deserted hospital lobby and were allowed to go upstairs to see George. I entered the room where he lay—not moving. Although his eyes were open, they appeared glazed over. I stared at him. I don't know why I did not hold him and kiss him—I was afraid. I will always regret that I did not try to speak to him, but I couldn't even gather my wits enough to formulate a thought before the hospital staff rushed me out of the room, saying "Something occurred and we have to operate immediately," that they were "getting the operating room ready, assembling staff, and stabilizing him." The surgeon told us that George was responsive and that he knew his name when asked. It was surreal.

From that moment on, the three of us wandered the eerily quiet hospital in the middle of the night waiting for the operation to be over. We allowed ourselves to be sheltered by assorted ugly waiting rooms, kindly aides offering blankets in an attempt to comfort and warm our bodies and spirits as we sat on cold plastic chairs—waiting, then perhaps moving on to another space. It was as if we were living in one of those nightmares where one walks through halls and mazes and cannot find a way out.

We were worried; it was taking a long time, and we had a bad feeling. We tried to cheer ourselves: He wasn't lying in the street somewhere; he was at a fine institution with talented and professional doctors and nurses caring for him. They would save him, wouldn't they? The same optimistic thought I had when Claudine was hospitalized so many years ago . . . well, sort of. This time, there was more than a fragment of fear.

We stared at the double doors from which we expected the doctor to emerge to tell us how George was. After many hours, as the sky turned rosy and then blue, we saw that the sun had risen on another gorgeous fall day. We waited for the outcome.

As light shone through the grimy windows, George was wheeled through the doors marked Do Not Enter with weary doctors accompanying him on either side of the gurney. That first glimpse of George was shocking. His body was swollen, and hideous tubes were keeping him alive.

# 8

# The Wait for George . . . 1992

**H**IS FACE AND BODY stunningly swollen as he emerged from the OR, George was handsome still. Doctors brazenly fed us "The Story." "The Story" told to us by the doctors and according to medical records was that "George's blood pressure was being artificially lowered with medication to decrease the pressure on the fragile tear in the aorta and the looming aortic dissection. Unfortunately, dissection progressed slowly then suddenly, without warning. The tear then advanced enough to allow blood to collect within the layers of the pericardial membrane, which surrounds the heart. The collection of blood teamed with a pericardial effusion that eventually led to a pericardial tamponade [the inability of the heart to beat efficiently enough due to increased surrounding pressure]. This led to anoxia [no oxygen to the brain] and subsequent cardiopulmonary arrest." Beating ceased for five, ten, or fifteen minutes. Doctors never admitted to the exact length of time he stopped breathing, only that he was rushed to the life-saving heart/lung machine.

"We are concerned about his waking up," the surgeon said when he finally spoke directly to us. Had their efforts been in time to rescue not only his heart but also his brain? Expressing concern, he said we would "just have to wait." Waiting was the name of this new chapter in our journey: twenty-four hours, then forty-eight hours, then longer. Waiting and watching over George in intensive care, we were allowed to enter the ICU every two hours, where we felt overwhelmed by unfamiliar apparatus and clear tubes with ugly colored liquid running through, the low hums and piercing clacking sounds of these peculiar devices keeping George alive. There were foul odors that sickened us. The foreign-feeling ICU cubicle was tiny and it hummed with sounds and our chatter.

After an exhausting day at George's side, I arrived home that second night of George's hospitalization and crumpled onto his side of the bed. I could not stop crying. That was my moment of truth. I remember thinking, *All is lost.* I knew then, no matter the words of hope given to us, no matter that hospital staff said they "didn't know what the outcome would be," no matter the prayers spoken and the cards received, the visitors who came to buoy me or talk to George, I knew all was lost. I knew it in the pit of my stomach. I knew he was not coming back. The words repeated in my head, *All is lost. All is lost.*

George did not die that tragic night, but for our little family it was an ending, and the beginning of a one-year-long strange and often desperate odyssey.

# 9

## It Isn't Over Yet . . . 1992

THROUGHOUT THE DAYS and nights we talked to George; relatives and friends talked, frantically trying to wake him. We peered at the doctors and nurses for answers, and hung on their every word. We searched their impassive faces; they looked away. They revealed little. Each day, we awoke with hope that perhaps this was the day George would turn the corner toward wakefulness.

The days grew cooler as they dragged on, and my sister, Josephine, and my girls celebrated my birthday at a somber dinner. It had been ten days since George fell ill. The next day, again, we persisted.

"Can a CAT scan be performed?" we queried.

"It's too soon, and he's hooked up to too many machines to be taken out of the unit," we were told.

Eyes became bleary watching the green bleeps measuring his steadily beating heart, and his blood pressure rising and falling. We gaped at the warnings, impatiently believing they would give us the answers we sought. More than a week after our request for more tests, they performed the first CAT scan. Moderate swelling indicated a brain insult. The surgical team tentatively relayed that George could come out of this; physically, his body was strong and healthy. A vague question as to whether we wanted to remove all machines was posed. "No," I said, "it's too soon."

Later, George was weaned off the respirator, and we were rewarded with a few moments of jubilation. They ventured to say that the swelling was not in the upper part of the brain, controlling thinking and reasoning.

It was peculiar watching the doctors coming and going, drinking coffee and Coke, living normally while our days were grim. Nothing seemed normal for us, and during this period of waiting, I often felt as if I were a witness, seeing myself and my family and friends as in a movie—a dreamlike reflection. More pictures of George's pitiable brain were taken, but because it was swollen, they could tell us little. Answers were painfully slow in coming as we begged for results and called countless times to obtain bits of information. Most of the hours passed with me feeling invisible. That was our new norm, until the day George left those walls.

I demanded a meeting with his doctors—the surgeon, the heart specialist, the neurologist, and the case manager—and so it was scheduled; it had now been almost two weeks since

George had spoken. Together with my older brother, Bob, my good friend Ruth, and George's brother Mike, I came armed with my carefully worded questions, itching to hurl them.

Sitting at the long shiny wood table in the unadorned conference room, I was beyond being intimidated. My look demanded answers, but this collection of clinicians could resolve nothing for me; their lame response was that they had decided to wait until the morning to operate so that a full complement of staff would be available. When this course had fallen apart because his condition deteriorated, they admitted to us, "Of course, it took time to prepare the operating room," and that "there was only one heart/lung machine." On this occasion, the surgeon actually admitted, "I could kick myself for not choosing to operate immediately." We were incredulous, asking why he could not pull together a full complement of staff in a big hospital like this University Hospital; we were stunned by his incredible response: "Well, you know, the hospital does have to close down."

The verdict emerged—almost a month after George's emergency surgery, when some of the swelling of his brain had subsided. George's brain had been hurt during the episode of his cardiac arrest, leaving the thinking and feeling part of his brain severely damaged, and what remained functioning was the brain stem—keeping George breathing, without knowing, feeling, thinking, speaking, eating, loving, or actually BEING.

This terrible diagnosis was given to us in bits and pieces, so we could digest it. Deep inside, I had been acutely aware of the truth from the beginning; on the nights following the operation, I had often seated myself awkwardly on George's side of the old double bed in our quiet bedroom. We had slept close together in that bed for the past twenty-seven years. Now it felt as though a knife had struck my heart. I feared all was indeed lost, that there might be no going back. Had the worst become reality, and would I forever after sleep without my George? Despair was setting in.

# 10

## Powerlessness and
## My Search for Truth . . . 1992/1993

AFTER MY INITIAL LEAVE just after the onset of
George's illness, I went back to work at my job as
administrative assistant at the Board of Education.
While at work, I went into action: I made calls to George's
school, to the union, to the welfare fund, to the retirement office,
and I cried. All the time, I cried. I continued to feel powerless
until I began to investigate exactly what happened to George
in the few short hours between the time we left him at the
hospital and the time we saw him emerging swollen and
sleeping from the operation.

I demanded answers and I demanded hospital records. It
was daunting, because the hospital administration put their
powerful procedures in the way of truth. I felt that my sorrow

and grief would only be transformed by becoming the power to find that truth. I waited edgily in various hospital offices, with sometimes less-than-helpful people, for the all-important records essential to my future. When I met with the hospital social worker, she couldn't understand my bitterness, and queried, "You blame Gus [the surgeon] for this tragedy?" I did.

George lay sleeping—or at least that is how he seemed, except for the gurgling in his throat. He was not sleeping! Initially, George had been in a coma, but as the days and weeks dragged by, they told us he was in a vegetative state, which meant that there had been a tragic insult to his brain. We never gave up on George. We played him a tape of our beloved dog Reddy Boy barking, and we talked to him incessantly, begging him to return. Although George made some involuntary facial grimaces and moved his eyes in sleep/wake cycles, valuable time had been allowed to be lost, and the operation on his ascending aortic aneurysm had come too late. The aorta had been repaired, and on the outside, George still appeared to be *sleeping.* I was powerless to change that.

My powerlessness had begun that first day in the hospital. The doctors, nurses, professionals had all the power. George was in their hands, and they had failed. Each day as I approached University Hospital, I paid strict attention to my driving, afraid I might crash if I didn't. I looked at the weather forecast, let the dog out, fed the cats, and dressed just like a normal person. If you saw me walking from the parking lot, I looked normal—I even put on my make-up and ate my breakfast. Life was all a blur, though—the blur of powerlessness. It was almost an out-of-body experience, watching myself performing the rituals of daily life. The only power I possessed was over these little daily tasks; the big power had already been lost.

Each day that I walked down the hospital hall, which smelled of cleaning fluids and bodily fluids, my stomach felt sick, and the power left my body. As I touched George each day, and even sometimes tried to lie down beside him in the bed, I was weak with sadness. One day blended into the next.

For many weeks, I dragged myself to his hospital room after work each and every evening, where his sad little cubicle greeted me with cheerful cards wishing George a "speedy recovery," or hollowly beseeching the gods to have mercy on George and return him to health. It was then that a second CAT scan was performed. The results were never reported to us by a neurologist, but the doctors on the case told us that things looked good and that the swelling had gone down; his surgeon said, "I can see no reason why he is not waking up." Of course, we were encouraged by statements like these. Our family was ecstatic for a moment or two. It was just a matter of time and he would wake up.

Our intense questioning begged further explanation of George's condition. Another fact was added: When he had been given the anesthesia, the blood pressure medicine and the anesthesia interacted lethally and caused the bleed-out to his heart and thus his brain. Several days after the surgery, he had been literally bombarded with steroids. They said, "We hit him with all we had in an effort to bring down the swelling in his brain." We longed for more, but there was nothing. Medically, they said, he was fine, but he was not waking from the coma.

Before long, however, the Head of Neurology at University Hospital revealed that the doctors had simply been avoiding the truth. Arriving at his office, my brother, Bob, my brother-in-law Mike, and I were cautiously hopeful while preparing ourselves for grave results. He gave his definitive conclusions. The CAT scan doesn't really tell you about brain damage; it just shows layers of the brain. There was no hope for George's recovery. Asked if George was suffering, the doctor replied, "George is not suffering, you are the only ones suffering." The reports confirmed that the latest EEG showed little brain activity, and there would probably be no meaningful recovery, unless there was a miracle. There was always that possibility. Of course, *that* was our only hope—a miracle.

Anger drove me to write a long letter to the surgeon who had operated on George. It was scathing, definitely pointing blame at him, and was meant to hurt and have him suffer the guilt I thought he should. Accusing him of never having had George's interest at heart, I said, "Your only interests were in convenience and schedules, and grave mistakes were made." The hospital and staff had been negligent. I continually asked the question, "How could your hospital not have the proper staff to mobilize and perform a serious operation for one person, with hours to spare?" The letter never found its way to the doctor or hospital, because I never mailed it.

Instead, my rage would be channeled toward more than blame: my new vocation was to investigate and procure the documents from their often-secret files, which would build the case of negligence into a future lawsuit against all the doctors involved in George's case, as well as the entire hospital community. Suddenly it became crystal clear. Here was my inspiration to get those lead feet moving each day. Feeling George beside me, and energized by my quest, I went forward. The truth would bring him home.

# 11

## Harry . . . The 1950s

I
N THE 1950S, WHEN I WAS seventeen or eighteen and
George and I were dating, he introduced me to the remarkable music and stage presence of Harry Belafonte.
We came to refer affectionately to Belafonte as "Harry," because
back in the time when he graced stages, nightclubs, and sta-
diums around the world, almost everyone knew who you were
talking about when you said, "Harry's at the Town and Country
Club," or "Harry's playing the Copa." Harry became important
to us and George took me to see Belafonte whenever he performed in New York.

We trudged uptown to see Harry at the great Lewisohn
Stadium at City College of New York (CCNY)—which for
decades was the performance venue for some of the great mu-
sicians of the world—we struggled against the throngs to our

seats high above the stage. Fans who were not able to get tickets to this concert gathered outside on the sidewalks of New York City to hear strains of Belafonte's music in open air.

We were privileged to see Harry perform at the cavernous Town and Country Club in Brooklyn on several occasions. When the lights were dimmed, the audience hushed—a single spotlight, clouded with smoke from the many cigarettes burning brightly, alighted on Harry's satin shirt and illuminated his strikingly gorgeous face.

At the infamous Copacabana in Manhattan, Harry sang his heart out for the packed house, where, at the tiny tables crowded together, men and women alike roared approval for his renditions of the joyful "Jamaica" and the soulful "Scarlet Ribbons," during which tears sprang to my eyes.

Harry was incredibly handsome and sexy; women undressed him with their eyes and drooled at his every wonderful movement. George and I were among his devoted fans; we owned all his albums.

I was thrilled to be reminded recently of our unique connection to Harry when one lonely evening—some forty years after my first introduction to the charismatic and talented musician— I tuned in to an amazing interview on public television. There sat Tavis Smiley across from still-handsome Harry Belafonte at the historic Lorraine Motel, now a museum dedicated to Dr. Martin Luther King, Jr. Harry had consented to this rare interview in honor of the anniversary of Dr. King's assassination. Harry was beloved and idolized, and I'm proud that George and I recognized him as the national treasure he was and is.

Another chapter in the George and Terri journey, as is the next detour.

# 12

# Life Changes . . . 1959

WHEN GEORGE WENT INTO the service in the late 1950s, everything changed for us. An exciting vacation to Miami Beach for me became a myriad of "firsts"—my first airplane trip, my first vacation as a young woman on my own, and my first affair. When I returned home at the end of the Miami Beach vacation—and after months of confusion as only a nineteen-year-old can suffer—I broke off the relationship with George and immersed myself in a new romance. Too young for a commitment, we both needed to grow up.

I remember Miami Beach in 1959. Sitting apprehensively at a tiny table in the Boom Boom Room, a dark, glitzy club in the legendary Fontainebleau Hotel, I never suspected my life would change forever that evening. My best friend, Ellen, and

I wore chic black dresses, hoping to meet young men and dance gaily on this, our first vacation away from our families. We were just out of high school and the glittering Miami Beach was glamorous beyond our wildest dreams. Ellen sipped vodka martinis, and I sipped white wine—always preferring eating to serious drinking.

It wasn't long before Ray, a handsome, charming man, asked me to dance. He said his name was Ramon, and that he was a dance instructor at the club. I wondered if perhaps he expected me to buy dance lessons. Instead, he pursued me that evening. Almost immediately, we spoke of books and psychology; later, he took me back to my hotel in his silver Porsche with a promise to meet me again the next day. I knew nothing of Porsches, nor did I realize how much older this man was. Responding only to his allure, I knew he was someone special.

Ray was true to his word—he picked me up at my hotel the next day. We spent hours on the warm sand and in the sparkling water. He gave me a tour of some of the more sensational hotels on the strip. Despite owning a Porsche, which he had undoubtedly purchased during his more financially flush years working long trips as a merchant seaman, Ray had little money, and I paid for lunch. We had dinner at a bar where they offered free hors d'oeuvres, and although we both drank little, we didn't have to buy our drinks because Ray was well known around town.

As the night grew deeper, Ray took me to his apartment, and there, in his cramped little room, we made love. It was my first time. We spent the rest of my vacation together, and one of our nights together culminated romantically with watching the sun rising over the shimmering ocean.

It was a whirlwind romance, and, as I look back, I was fortunate that he was not a murderer or a drug dealer. Young and naïve, I discovered Ray to be a self-taught man of intelligence and quality, possessing the highest morals. Later, as years passed, I came to know him as a mature adult, and my view of his character never wavered. He never lied to me, and as he often said of me, he "rang true."

## More About Ray . . . 1959

A T THE END OF MY two-week vacation, I left Miami Beach with a breaking heart and Ray's promise ringing in my ear—he would be coming to New York in a few weeks. He told me he was a merchant seaman and that he needed to ship out from New York; he would see me soon. To my delight, several weeks later, Ray arrived in New York, Porsche and all. I was away for the weekend at Point Pleasant in New Jersey. Not having cell phones at the time, I have no idea how he tracked me down to telephone the shabby furnished beach apartment I was staying in. He convinced me to take the train back to Manhattan to meet him. My heart beat wildly as I left my friends and returned to NYC on the railroad. Ray met me at Grand Central Station and we spent the weekend in Greenwich Village at his brother's apartment.

When Ray went off to do one of his long stints in the Merchant Marines—or, as he referred to it, when he "shipped out"—he didn't leave me alone. Besides wooing me from afar with postcards from around the globe, he left me the car that had—sadly—replaced his Porsche, which he had sold because he needed the money. It was a white convertible Volkswagen Beetle (the "Bug"). Even though I didn't know how to drive a

Ray in Greenwich Village

stick shift, Ray had supreme confidence that I would be able to drive. So drive I did—without trepidation and with just a little fear, I drove, stalled, drove, and stalled all over Manhattan and Queens until I got the hang of it.

I did get the hang of it, and went on to be a great stick-shift driver, even able to teach my own daughter to do the same. I have not driven a stick shift in many years, but I know I would be able to get right back in the saddle soon enough.

I still find this recollection exciting and I'm fortunate to call it my own—and to be able to tell my sweet grandchildren about it. In this year of 2013, I'm hopeful they'll think me "cool."

Ray was worldly—I met him as a suave dance instructor, but he also had a life as a licensed First Mate in the Merchant Marines. Through our discussions, he taught me about psychology; he introduced me to Latin dancing and took me to Harlem to dance to the music of Tito Puente. He was an exciting companion and we explored Manhattan together from the Upper West Side to the cobblestone streets of Greenwich Village. To me, he was a cross between Jack London and Sigmund Freud.

At that time, Ray seemed like the love of my life—but our love story would never be written completely; instead, it was a breathtaking and life-changing interlude.

Almost three years later, and after rivers of tears, Ray convinced me that I must go on with my life, get married, have children, and live a lovely solid existence. It was Ray, after all, who became the first to encourage me to call George to perhaps rekindle our relationship. Ray knew he could not be the husband and father I needed to make my life complete.

## More Memories of Miami Beach ... Then and Now

E VEN THOUGH RAY had sent me on my way, I would have none of it and made a rash decision to follow him to Miami Beach. But I was young and it was to be an adventure. My mom, my maiden aunt, Concetta—who, by the way, I always feared I'd end up like—and my Uncle Phil, a favorite of mine, accompanied me to Miami Beach. We took the train down, and stayed at an elegant hotel; we were on vacation, and then, after a week, they went home. Before our teary parting, Uncle Phil helped me find an apartment. It was a charming, bright studio in a private house in the somewhat rundown South Beach area of Miami Beach. Sarah, the owner of the house, was a Jewish lady with a European accent and a bird's nest of bleached blond hair offsetting heavily lined, tanned skin. She loved the sun.

Sarah rented rooms to elderly people; she took care of these old people, preparing their meals and conducting Shabbos on Friday evenings. She and I loved each other from the beginning; she enjoyed having me around, and sometimes I joined the family at Friday night services. Her favorite thing to say to me with her special Yiddish inflection was, "You could be a Jewish girl." Her own daughter had moved away to attend college, and now lived in Minneapolis. Sarah knew I was looking for a job, and she heard that Abe Gefter, owner of the kosher hotel the Cromwell, was looking for a secretary—and so, a match was made. The only hitch was that I had to agree to work there for the entire season, until June, when the hotel closed for the summer. I agreed.

At one point during the winter season, my room at Sarah's house had to be rented to someone who could pay the going price, which was higher than I was able to pay. Moving to a miniature bedroom apartment with windows all around (I don't recall that it even had a kitchen) made it seem like I was living in a tree house. When Sarah saw it, she was horrified, and she asked me to come back; she had a room belonging to her daughter that she never rented, but for me, "the little Jewish girl," it would be just fine. We became very close, and often went to the beach together, or she let me drive her around in her big old Cadillac station wagon.

Soon after arriving at the Cromwell, I met Ruth, the front desk girl there. She also operated the hotel's ancient telephone switchboard, the old-fashioned type with the long snaky chords that plugged into corresponding holes. Ruth was a young Jewish girl from England immigrating to America; she was to stay with family friends in Miami Beach. She was an orphan, looking for a new life in the States. We became instant friends.

Ruth and I made friends with Beatrice, a lively Columbian girl, who lived with her mother and sister. Beatrice usually had to be chaperoned when she went out—it was the custom. But her mom allowed her to go out with me, because I was a "good girl." I couldn't believe how wild Beatrice became when we were out of her mother's view!

Ruth and I met all Beatrice's Columbian and Cuban friends, vivacious boys and girls who loved to party. I met an adorable nineteen-year-old young man named Roberto, and we had fun dancing, and yes, romancing. He certainly took my mind off Ray and I felt like a normal young woman, dating someone nearer my own age. Sadly for me because I missed him, Roberto eventually adhered to his parents' wishes and left Miami Beach to attend Louisiana State University to become an engineer. He and I wrote to each other regularly, and several years later we met again in California, when I went out West to visit Ruth (at that time she was living in Los Angeles); Roberto and I shared a sentimental and romantic weekend reunion. I have often wondered since what happened to him!

The year in Miami Beach was filled with parties and Latin dancing under moonlit skies. It was the 60s, and many Cuban professionals had found their way to the region, with former doctors, dentists, and businessmen now working as elevator operators and waiters at the hotel. I was immersed in both Latin life and Jewish life, and reveled in both, expanding my horizons and enjoying the varied colorful influences of each. The mambo with its heart-stopping beat, the delicious yellow rice *paella,* and the lyrical Spanish words I came to love were wonderful. Then there were the Jewish traditions, the candles on Friday night, the tasty chopped liver, and the Gefilte fish I couldn't put in my mouth—all these experiences and flavors added up to an education of the highest order.

My life was full of fun in Miami Beach, and I only saw Ray on several occasions. I was distancing myself and becoming accustomed to life without him—understanding, finally, that I had to move on.

All too soon, the Miami Beach season was over, and Ruth and I were winging north; Ruth, on her way to the Catskill Mountains for the summer season there, and I, home to my parents. Ruth was following her love, an Israeli busboy she had fallen for. I bravely drove on my own to the Catskill Mountains, where I visited Ruth at work and experienced first-hand the dingy but exciting life of the young people who worked the popular Catskill resorts depicted in the film *Dirty Dancing.* The visit there sparked a recollection of the time a couple of years earlier when I had gone to Grossinger's Hotel to apply for a job as secretary to Jenny Grossinger. Ray had heard about this position, and we drove up together for my interview. I didn't get the job, because the interviewer asked, "Are you

willing to live here in the mountains, away from your family?"
She instinctively gathered from my vague response that the
answer was *No*. Little did I know that a year later I would leave
everything to follow Ray to Miami Beach!

At the end of the summer season in the mountains, Ruth
and I rented an apartment together in Jackson Heights, NY
and our Miami Beach adventure was over, for the moment.
We soon parted to live our separate lives, each of us going on
to marry and start our families.

But this important relationship forged out of that adventure
remained. To this day, Ruth and I speak weekly on the phone,
even though she lives in California. We have visited each other
many times over the years and vacation together frequently. I
can never forget that Ruth was my rock when George got sick,
staying with me for several weeks during the nightmarish year
just after George was hospitalized and throughout the lonely
days surrounding my daughter's wedding.

Ray and I never ceased to be friends. He telephoned from
time to time to check on me, and once we met in Central Park;
I was eager to show him my cherubic new baby girl snuggled
in her pram. Much later, when my girls were teenagers, he
talked to me from NYU Hospital, where he was in hospice,
dying from cancer. The young woman currently in his life, an
artist, was caring for him, and I was glad he was not alone.
Using Ray's given name to refer to him after he died, his
brother Arnold called me, "Could you come over to collect
some lovely old photos that Justus kept and wanted you to
have?" I told George about the phone call and he drove me to
Arnold's apartment at One Fifth Avenue to gather the bits and
pieces. Of course, I still hold them dear.

In the spring of 2007, Ruth and I and her husband, Manny—the busboy, now a plumber—had a grand reunion in Miami Beach. We wanted to return to the happy times we had spent in Florida, and to see how our little paradise had turned to the grandiose South Beach, now populated with fancy condominiums and luxurious hotels where old run-down apartments for the elderly escaping from the cold of the North had been. We were able to locate some of the edifices that had been there in the sixties—including, of course, the Fontainebleau, as well as one of the smaller hotels where Ray and I had watched the sun rise so many years ago.

We found Gefter's Cromwell Hotel where we all had worked; it had morphed into an opulent Grecian structure designed in an all-white motif. Candles softly illuminated every corner. The actual building was still there, and we were thrilled to find it still intact. Ruth and Manny and I amazed everyone we met when we told them that we had become friends there in Miami Beach more than forty years prior.

With that visit, I felt I had come full circle in my Miami Beach connection. It may be fun to visit again with my children and grandchildren—or maybe not. It might be more fun to keep the secrets of the white sand and moonlit skies to myself.

# 13

## The Fairytale Continues
## . . . 1965/1966

### "Try to Remember"

*Try to remember the kind of September*
*When life was slow and oh, so mellow.*
*Try to remember the kind of September*
*When grass was green and grain was yellow.*
*Try to remember the kind of September*
*When you were a tender and callow fellow,*
*Try to remember, and if you remember, then follow.*

*Try to remember when life was so tender*
*That no one wept except the willow.*
*Try to remember when life was so tender*
*That dreams were kept beside your pillow.*
*Try to remember when life was so tender*

*That love was an ember about to billow.*
*Try to remember, and if you remember, then follow.*

*Deep in December, it's nice to remember*
*Although you know the snow will follow.*
*Deep in December it's nice to remember*
*Without a hurt the heart is hollow.*
*Deep in December, it's nice to remember*
*The fire of September that made us mellow.*
*Deep in December our hearts should remember, and follow.*

M Y EXPERIENCE WITH RAY was magical, but would lead me to the "real" joyous life with George and our children. I believe the break was a blessing for George, too; the challenge and loss of our relationship helped him grow up. George was to become my rock, my best friend—he was destined to be the love of my life.

The miracle of our break-up was that we had both remained unmarried for all these years. He was from the old neighborhood, so I happened to see him at a local club, and he looked adorable. My sister-in-law Marie suggested I just call him at home. I did, and when we met again, we were ready for a life together. It was so easy and natural, as though we knew someday we would wind up together.

Our wedding was true storybook as I reminisce about that warm July day just two days before George's birthday. Our reception at the picturesque Ripples on the Water—a kind of peculiar name for Oscar Hammerstein's estate in Beechhurst, New York—was nestled in the shadow of the Throgs Neck Bridge. In this charming landmark-designated

A precious time—we're engaged

building, we danced with loving eyes of both our families looking on.

The character of this stunning old mansion—with its windows peeking out at the bridge and onto the harbor below, and with sailboats appearing tiny and sparkling in the sun—made the day enchanting. Another white dress—this one a sheer organdy wedding gown—played an important role, as had the white dress of so many years ago. Our wedding song, "Try to Remember," had been special to us in those early days. Now, in the present, as I think of the song in my grief and sorrow, I find it poignant. The words haunt me, because that is what I have had to do, always, *try to remember.* We savored every moment of our wedding day, and went on to an idyllic honeymoon in Bermuda. We were beginning our fairytale life, and we were happy.

A Valentine for me from George at the beginning of our marriage:

> There is a word I'd like to say
> On this very special Valentine's Day.
>
> Even bad as I may be,
> Your love is there plain to see.
>
> Although I always cause you pain,
> You play and pet me just the same.
>
> You worry so when I'm sick,
> To Dr. Kopp you take me quick.
>
> And when I'm well, all is joy;
> You're so happy for your boy.
>
> You feed me first before you eat,
> With tasty dishes that are a treat.
>
> And I hope to behave some day.
> And all your goodness try to repay.
> ~Thumps [the dog]

# 14

# Honeymoon in Bermuda . . . 1966

GEORGE AND I SPENT the first night of our married life at a hotel near Kennedy Airport, which at that time was named Idlewild Airport. The hotel had been informed that we were newlyweds, and a bottle of champagne and fresh fruit awaited us. We would be leaving for our honeymoon early the next morning. As was the custom in 1966, I was dressed in a summery white dress-and-coat ensemble chosen for the occasion; George's brother and his family arrived at the hotel excitedly the next morning in order to drive us to the nearby airport to catch our early-morning flight, taking many obligatory photos.

Then, we were off! As luck would have it, we were bumped up to first class, and enjoyed an elegant flight, which we shared with the three-term former NYC Mayor Wagner and his wife,

Terri and George

who happened to be on the same plane. We were served filet mignon, shrimp, and more champagne. It could not have been more exciting.

We landed in Hamilton, Bermuda and then took a long taxi ride to the other end of this tropical island to our destination: Cambridge Beaches. It was worth the ride. The place was secluded, each patron occupied their own cottage—a romantic breakfast was served to us each day in ours—and tasteful meals were enjoyed in the glass-enclosed dining room overlooking the sea.

We honeymooned for two weeks. We rode bikes to explore, took superb picnic lunches prepared just for us and rowed boats around the inlets, and visited the charming towns that dotted this lovely island. We were mesmerized by an evening spent with the local people who were celebrating a festival—we were the only tourists there, and we walked back to our hotel under a warm moonlit sky. And to make things even more interesting, we recognized Hume Cronyn and Jessica Tandy (with their dog) in one of the adjoining cottages. An unforgettable honeymoon.

Just to tell how crazy we both were about animals and our dog Oliver in particular, as we walked back to our cottage in the evening or during our explorations in the early morning, we saw dozens of little frogs, and they reminded us of our dog. We were more than ready to go home to begin our life together.

## Just for the Record . . .
## Our Romance Through the Years

EXCITEMENT BETWEEN George and me had begun when I was sixteen and he was twenty-one, with long kisses in the hallway downstairs from the second-floor apartment I shared with my family in the old neighborhood in L.I.C. That excitement continued years later with stolen hours of romance—from the apartment I shared with my brother during the months of courtship between George and me, to the top floor of the rustic cabin in Vermont on a snowy morning when our friends had gone to church.

When we were on our honeymoon, we enjoyed each other on the warm sands in Bermuda in the secret and secluded cove that could only be reached by our own little motorboat.

All that was only the beginning; I wouldn't say it was always marital bliss, but throughout our years together we had fun, and made sure romance was never far from us— most of the time.

# 15

## Persistent Vegetative State
... 1992/1993

G EORGE'S ILLNESS DROVE ME to investigate everything related to this calamity. My bizarre and often
poignant journey took me into a world where some
patients and families live—for me, the world of the vegetative
state was born.

We clung to George's bedside and gazed questioningly at
him. Sometimes it was just the girls and me, and Mike and
Paul, and at other times, close friends stood by. George's brothers and his nephew were loyal in coming to stand by the bed
to encourage him.

Gazing at the unnatural scenes sliding before my eyes
daily, I became aware of a strange phenomenon: I was uncomfortable in George's presence—not at all when we were alone,
but with a roomful of people at the bedside, or with friends

who were acquaintances. We were peeking in on a very private space. It seemed irreverent.

Looking around at the faces, and becoming aware of people talking to each other—actually talking over George—I wanted to scream, "Get out! Go home! We're here for George or, at least, to comfort me. Please be respectful in this room."

Along with these feelings, there was a stab of embarrassment about George's condition. It was a curious condition, and no one wants to be so different. It wasn't a heart attack or even cancer—it was a vegetative state. Rarely able to speak those words until the honest writing of these pages, I have confronted the uneasiness. Fun is often made of this label; people are referred to as "vegetables," a repugnant way to describe a person; it has an ugly connotation. The nuance is shame, as though we did something wrong, and were punished. The sorry state of his poor, hurt brain was the farthest thing from normal; persistent vegetative state can be dark and chilling.

Thoughts of guilt surfaced, too—thinking of the times in the past when I thought George wasn't taking care of himself and I had said, jokingly, "I won't take care of you when you're old and decrepit; you'll have to go to a nursing home." He hated being sick—it made him vulnerable and weak, and he rarely succumbed to illness. Now he was at his most vulnerable—in this vegetative state.

Confiding to my journals my guilt about putting the animals to sleep when they were old and sick came to me; somehow I felt I was being punished for these deeds. At my lowest ebb, I found remorse in everything I've ever done. Fault somehow goes hand in hand with this thing—this "vegetative state."

For some solace and peace, my investigations took me to documented vegetative state cases, some of the more famous being Nancy Cruzan and Karen Ann Quinlan. I acquired a tape of a public television special that documented *The Life and Death of Nancy Cruzan*. It was riveting and heartbreaking to view, but I forced myself to watch so I could learn. I stared at Nancy; she looked exactly as George did, with her wake and sleep cycles, and with her family talking to her as if she could hear, celebrating her birthdays. I cried for her parents, her sister, her family. After eight long years, they had won their case for her right to die, and she was released. Her parents and sister created a foundation in her name and participated in another documentary about the right to die and other bioethical issues, which I studied and gained strength from. Her father took his own life several years later and the foundation was disbanded.

I spoke personally to Nancy's family on several occasions, and also met more than once with a young woman from Little Neck, whose young husband had been in the same condition as George. The outcomes were always the same. There was no coming back for these unfortunates.

There are other cases, not as famous. I spoke to several families personally, needing desperately to talk to people who had been through a situation such as mine; they were so kind, so helpful, and only they knew what I was going through. I came away with the strong belief that there should be a support group for loved ones of those suffering this condition and for those seeking to remove life support, fighting to let these poor souls die with dignity, if the family so chose. Family members need to hear about the stages of despair, the questions that come up, and the guilt.

Several of the family members I consulted appealed to the courts to remove the feeding tubes from their loved ones. Writing to a doctor in Minnesota, a renowned expert in this field, I obtained articles and opinions from him about cases he was involved in. He ventured to say he was sure there was no hope of recovery in George's case. We were moving toward removing the feeding tube, as George might live as he was for some years, although at his age, it was not likely that he would live more than five more years. But I knew that George would not have wanted to live this way—and nor, for that matter, would I.

A plan was revealed to me. I would wait a year before requesting that the feeding tube be removed. If there had been no meaningful improvement by then, I would let him die.

# 16

## Fear and Getting Lost . . . 1992

'VE BEEN LOST MANY TIMES in my life. Early in my driving career, when I was just a youngster, I was fearless when driving to the Bronx to visit my cousins, or to the far reaches of Brooklyn, where I knew nothing about the unfamiliar neighborhoods, or even into congested, taxi-clogged Manhattan streets.

But I always got lost!

Of course, there were no GPS systems then and often the directions I received left a lot to be desired—or my interpretation thereof was faulty. But there was no fear. Just inquiries along the way: "How do I get to 15th Street?" or, "Where is Ocean Parkway?" or, just a drop into a gas station. I had confidence.

When I was in my twenties, I drove up to the Catskill Mountains to visit my friend Ruth during the time she was working at a popular resort.

I got lost.

So what? There was no fear attached to that experience. I got there after a few detours.

After George and I married and had children, when we stayed at a rented cottage high in the mountains, often he didn't want to leave the dogs or a comfy chair, so off the children and I would go to a country fair, or to the movies—out into the blackest night on dark roads without a hint of light, as only country roads can be.

We may have gotten lost, but eventually we found our way. I was not afraid.

Then, years later, I began to feel desperately lost. In the first few months of George's hospitalization when I left the house, keys in hand, and plunged into the night darkness, I felt fear. Cautiously, I would enter my cold car, beginning even a brief journey with trepidation.

Once I had made an appointment to meet some of the women from a support group at one of their homes. The home was in Flushing.

I lived in Flushing. The woman's house was less than twenty blocks away.

Abandonment and dread gripped me. Fearing I would get lost and be unable to find my way, I realized I *was* lost, and the feeling overwhelmed me, as my brain searched for the familiar. I pushed on, got in the car, turned on the ignition. I slowly drove the streets—the few side streets to my destination. But as I drove there, I felt as though I were traveling on mysterious roads in the middle of a bleak, shadowy night—alone.

Even as I ran the few steps from the car to the house I was visiting, I looked behind me: was I safe? This scene repeated itself whenever I went to any of the women's homes. I was always looking behind me, fearful.

Fearful and lost.

It would be some time until I drove on highways at night, even though I had been driving on highways at night since I was eighteen. The fear of being lost had developed with the grief of missing George—I was lost in his illness, and the grief had overtaken me.

I was fortunate that my friend Connie often accompanied me on my sojourns away from home. Many times my daughters or my darling brother-in-law Mike (George's brother), or my own brother, Bob, traveled with me. Whether it was to visit with George in the nursing home or to consult an attorney about George's case, I usually had welcomed company.

I was adrift because of this emotional loss, a disturbing "being lost" intertwined with George being absent because of his illness. I was lost from what had been.

But somehow I did not feel lost or fearful as I approached the offices in the hospital where I attempted to find out details of George's hospitalization at University Hospital in September of 1992. There, I was mentally driven and fearless. No lost little lady there—only a strong woman attempting to find out exactly what happened when she left her husband in a place he should have been safe.

Many a night I railed and raved at George and at God, asking, "Why is this happening?" Once, and only once—although the moment is etched in my brain—the sinister thought crept into my consciousness as I drove along a gloomy street:

*How easy and fine it would be just to drive into the oncoming embankment; it would be all over and I wouldn't have to feel the pain.*

No, how cowardly—what about the people and pets who loved me, a few of whom had not even been born yet? After long months, fears eased, and I began to taste once more the sweetness of waking up each morning and going about the daily routines of home and work. Still, grieving deeply, I voraciously read books and articles about death and the afterlife, as though George were already dead. He was gone to me.

Ironically, during the first few months of George's illness, grief support groups would not accept me, because George was not dead. The coma recovery support group met once a week at the hospital, but when I entered the starkly plain meeting room, I didn't know what felt more horrifying: learning about the sad states of the patients who were at various stages of consciousness and coma recovery, or recognizing the fact that George would never reach those states. This support group was not for me; I did not belong there.

I made an exhaustive search, but no support group existed for those caring for patients in a persistent vegetative state. These patients were hidden away, as were their families. I did locate a gentleman in our area, whose wife had fallen into this state. She had been living in a nursing home for the past five years. I skulked around the store he owned, hoping to talk to him. Never finding the courage to speak to him about his painful vigil, I knew I might live years standing by George's bedside as he had for his wife in the nursing home. I spoke to one of his children; she just shook her head and kept saying, "It's too long—too long."

I can report to others who may experience similar feelings of being lost that, as time passed, I was once again able to venture out, to drive away from my neighborhood and travel out of my comfort zone. I no longer felt as lost as I once had. After some time, and after George had been laid to rest, that feeling of not being lost grew—and, in time, I was found.

# 17

# George's Work
# . . . 1950s and Beyond

A FTER HIGH SCHOOL, George had begun his career as a tool and die maker (a machinist) and apprenticed at an ancient shop beneath the apartment he shared with his family. Here George found his niche—he excelled at the precision it required; he was good with his hands.

In time he became partners with a friend and bought the shop. He was now a "big typhoon," as he would often joke. But being boss was not for him. Uncomfortable with that role, he sold his share of the business and took a job at a local factory. Then a stroke of luck came his way, luck that would change his life and add to his contentment: the civil service test for machinist. George and machinist would make a perfect fit. His name was added to the rolls of city workers.

George was assigned to Brooklyn Automotive High School in that eclectic and fascinating borough. Automotive was a special school—the only one of its kind belonging to the New York City Board of Education. He adored that historical old building. He served the school for twenty years, and was proud when he helped the kids.

He loved his job at Automotive. He could not believe his good fortune—to have a job he prized, with many friends to share the hours spent at work; all the wonderful vacation time, holidays off; a regular workday with no midnight hours, and health benefits, too. George was often heard saying, "God bless the Board of Education."

# 18

## Divine Intervention . . . 1973

I N 1973, OUR YOUNG FAMILY—George and me, and our two daughters aged two and five—were living in a small four-room apartment in Queens on a busy street. We dreamed of owning a house to call our own.

Neither George nor I had ever lived in a home of our own; both families had always rented. It was going to be our dream come true. It would be a new and exciting chapter in our lives—the chapter that would make the fairy tale complete. We had two dogs, after all, and they needed to be walked at least twice a day; we wanted a yard for them and a green space for our girls, complete with swing set and maybe an above-ground pool.

We had little money for a down payment, but we persevered in saving what we could. Suddenly, George found himself in a position to make extra money. He was offered the chance to produce some specific designs in the tool and die trade, one section at a time, for which he would be paid thousands of dollars each. He precisely produced each intricate part after regular business hours at the shop where he worked. Although he often worked late into the night, his hard work and my evenings spent alone with the children were sacrifices we both enthusiastically made.

I played my part in the scheme too. He often instructed me to go out and purchase various materials he needed to complete the item. I would take the baby and go off to unusual small and often dirty shops, where I obtained the unique bits and pieces he needed. Descriptions of the exact measures of metal that were required were described on a sheet of paper; I had no clue as to what they were. If one shop didn't have the item, I was off to another.

"I couldn't have done it without you," George gratefully told me. "You were crucial to the operation." This specialized work lasted for exactly one year, and no longer. The job was completed and no more after-hours money would come our way. The amount saved had been just enough for the down payment; this unique opportunity had been divine intervention and we could now begin the search for our dream home.

Christine was now six, so she put in her requests: she wanted stairs to her bedroom, a garage, and—of course—a yard. We wanted to remain in Queens, so we searched Flushing, Bayside, Whitestone, and Douglaston. We found our dream home in Flushing, near Bayside. It was perfect to us, it fulfilled all of Christine's requirements, and George loved it too. It had a huge basement where he could build and fix until

Our family home

the wee hours of the morning if he wished. It was at least forty years old—not nearly new—but it had not been abused, and we could make lovely changes to our old "new look."

We lived in that home in mostly peaceful harmony for many years. I continue to live joyfully in our old "new house," and I can't believe it has been thirty-four years since we crossed its threshold.

Now the children are gone, and the grandchildren enjoy the space. They play a mean game of hide-and-seek in all the many interesting spots it affords them. I have lived there with many pets over the years; as I write this book, I am down to four cats. Often it seems too large, as my children remind me—and I ponder the idea of seeking out a new look once more. I admire the lovely condominiums that are brand new and sparkling. *They are too far out on Long Island or in Westchester,* I tell myself. *I still have pets,* I tell myself. *I love my neighbors,* I tell myself. *I like being near the railroad into the City,* I tell myself.

In truth, I am so comfortable in my lovely old home. And so I ponder on . . . I am not ready to give my life a different "new look" than the one I signed on to so long ago. Maybe someday, but not today.

# 19

## Trouble in Paradise
## . . . The Late 1970s

Bleak times surfaced in our marriage, and during those times, black clouds colored our days. With two young children, two dogs, a mortgage, and endless bills, we were unfulfilled and angry. We fought, and that hostility drove us to marriage counseling—quite another miracle. Here was George, a middle-class, blue-collar man, and he agreed to spill his guts to a stranger. He was surprised and touched one evening when, after a huge fight, I said, "George, I want to save our marriage more than anything in the world." He hadn't known how strongly I felt. He said, "Okay, make the appointment." He truly loved the children and me, so he said, "I'll do what it takes."

We were referred to Dr. Crandall, a minister/marriage counselor near our home. Embracing the idea of therapy was not new to me—I reveled in it—but George's willingness wavered. Our first visit, I felt I had dragged George to the appointment kicking and screaming; we were hostile toward each other and George was unsure about his faith in this process. We tentatively entered Dr. Crandall's cramped little office, overflowing with books and papers, but Dr. Crandall's first query—"Tell me why you fell in love with each other"—opened the dialogue. My initial skepticism about seeing a minister transformed as I soon realized that Dr. Crandall was gifted in his field. George was not as easily won over, however. He once told a friend, "Sometimes we arrive for our sessions hand in hand, but by the time we depart, we utter not a word on the way home."

At first, we blamed each other's families for our despair, and aired our anger about who didn't do enough around the house, and who was belligerent and moody. Once, George—in such a fit of anger—was so upset that he left our home in Flushing and walked all the way to Brooklyn Automotive High School without telling me where he was going. Scared and worried—there were no cell phones then—I called my friend Connie, crying and wondering where he was. Was this to be a final break? He appeared at home hours later that night—his shoes practically worn through. We weren't finished yet.

Once that surprising commitment to therapy was made, George went—not cheerfully, but he went—and gradually, our work with Dr. Crandall began to turn our marriage around. My heart was proud that George, who refused to read any of the self-help books or articles I put in front of him, came with me to counseling every week, month after month. He was

Terri, all grown up

brave to travel this journey with me. It was daunting. Exploring our grievances hour by hour took time and patience. It was an important crossroad in our lives. After some two years—and one rescued cat (found just outside of the counselor's office)—later, we left our weekly talking cure, ready to face future problems on our own.

## To My Wife

The winter is over, at last, and we look forward
    to its end,
The cold that chilled us to the bone, the frosty gusts
    that make trees bend,

Our hands and feet have seen such pain, caused
    by frigid chill,
The depressing sight of long raw nights,
With the sound of howling windy shrill.

And now we look forward to the best—
To the warmth of summer's gift,

The sun that shines so bright, the joys that await,
    cannot be too swift.

But my real prize that I treasure most is with me
    all year through,
The presence of a lasting love—the one I share
    with you.

                        Love always,
                        George

# 20

## Before Trouble in Paradise

B EFORE TROUBLE IN PARADISE, there had been paradise. After our storybook wedding, George and I eagerly embarked on our next adventure: babies. Within the first year of our story, we welcomed our first daughter, a beautiful baby girl we named Christine. Three years later, the three of us—and the dog—welcomed our second daughter, Claudine (who was named by George).

After experiencing that serious bump in the road when Claudine suffered her life-threatening accident, the years tumbled by. We seemed energized and determined to treasure every moment of our lives as a family. Although we had longed for a home of our own, our inexpensive four-room apartment in Long Island City had been perfect, and both of our families were nearby. We often gathered at Grandma Mary's—George's mother's—apartment for Sunday dinners, were with Grandma Rose and Grandpa Rocco—my parents—for sleepovers, or had grand picnics sheltered by a lean-to with my sister and brother and their children at Pound Ridge Reservation in Pound Ridge, NY, where we communed with nature. We thought life was paradise.

After we moved to our wonderful old house in Flushing—with two growing daughters and two dogs—life seemed a jumble of activities and parties, parties, parties. Most parties were celebrated in the big backyard—birthday parties joyfully celebrated in April and May, First Holy Communion parties, Confirmation parties, graduation celebrations, and more, all took place there.

Two parties deserve a special look-back:

Especially sweet to recall was the occasion when Christine, only nine, (and Claudine, only six) decided they would throw us a tenth-year-anniversary party. With Connie's help (she lived next door), Chrissi sent out invitations to close family and friends, and somehow managed food, cake, and McDonald King-and-Queen hats, which we were implored to wear—so let the party begin. Of course it was a "surprise" and the most adorable aspect of this unique and marvelous celebration was that the guests—along with George and me, the surprise-ees—were asked to climb the stairs to the girls' brightly painted yellow bedroom for the festivities. It was the only room with air conditioning, and the cute pictures of George and me there in our "hats" are precious.

Another memorable party was George's "surprise" fiftieth birthday, planned by the girls and me and held at a VFW hall. I'm overjoyed that George got to feel the love and admiration of our families, good friends, and his "card-club buddies" in the light of the tragedy that would befall him only eight short years later.

It was during these years that George and I joined neighborhood friends in our valiant fight to save our neighborhood school, only two blocks from our home. We held rallies, stopped traffic on the busy Francis Lewis Boulevard, descended on the local school board, and met in the diner to discuss strategies. George was completely supportive and took care of the girls while I continued with the fight, and when he was required, he showed up with a twenty-five-foot ladder to hang a much-needed sign on the school building. We lost the fight to save the school, but forged lasting friendships, which I am the beneficiary of—to this day.

We believed in vacations, and even when there was little money, we managed to "get away" even if for just a few days, and most vacations included our two dogs. It was pure glee when we rented a home in the Pocono Mountains, packed up dogs and kids, and sat by the fireplace or played in the pools and streams.

At long last, a big vacation: We were going to Disney World in Orlando and Busch Gardens in St. Petersburg, Florida. It was "hot as hell" but a joy. We, however, experienced pleasure every day during the summer months in our own backyard because we had a pool. This aboveground model was a cool respite for all the kids in the neighborhood. Dozens of children learned to swim in that pool, including our dear Daniela, who lived next door, so many years later. It was a pool in which George and I allowed ourselves some quiet time in the dark of night, as we submerged ourselves in the cool water, kids asleep upstairs.

There were more paradise-like days for George and me and our kids—or with just George and me: we actually spent a romantic weekend at Paradise Stream in the Pocono Mountains when we wanted to recapture early magical moments.

George especially delighted in our Girl Scout camping weekend, where he was the life of the party—helpful, social, strong, and a good dad to any of the kids who might need him: a portrait of George.

# 21

## Farm Vacations . . . Around 1980

WE BECAME EXPERTS on farm vacations. We soon found ourselves wondering where else we would spend a special week's vacation!

We all loved animals. There were no computers then, so how did I come to find Elm's Farm in the Catskill Mountains and The Inn at East Hill Farm in Troy, New Hampshire? I can't remember—newspapers? Magazines? Chambers of Commerce? However, I did it, I found them, and we loved those precious weeks on farms.

Kittens, a dog, horseback riding, bunnies, goats, cows to milk, and a haystack to slide down at Elm's Farm were all stuff of a child's dream, and our children were no different. For George and I, wholesome meals—much of it grown on nearby farms or on the farm on which we stayed—were included. The farm also boasted boating, fishing, arts and crafts—and who could have summer vacation without a pool? A pool or lake was a must for us, as we all loved to swim.

The Inn at East Hill Farm was a little different. It was a "resort farm." It included entertainment, shuffleboard, and interesting scheduled activities every day: hayrides, cookouts, volleyball, and baseball. The highlight of the week was a serious climb up Mount Monadnock. George and I triumphantly did it, and we have the certificate and photograph of us at the top to prove it. Our girls were about ten and thirteen, and did not make it to the summit on this trip—but they got another chance.

# And . . . 2008

FAST-FORWARD OUR LIVES almost thirty years to find the magic of the Inn at East Hill Farm in New Hampshire once more. My little family—Chrissi, Mike, Claudy, Paul, Zack, Alyssa, Danielle, Luke, Alexandra—and I sped up through the beautiful Green Mountains to vacation at the Farm. Sadly, we were without George.

This time I didn't climb the mountain, but the Inn at East Hill had added a welcome cocktail party, air conditioning, and more spacious and elegant sleeping rooms, which were charming. The old ambiance still remained, and thoughts of George flooded back from the time we had vacationed there together.

The kids tried waterskiing and mountain climbing, as well as canoeing and rowing on the gorgeous lake. There was no end to the children's delight as they collected eggs for our

Grammy's/Mimi's Babes:
Alexandra, Zack, Mimi/Grammy, Danielle, Luke, and Alyssa

breakfasts, held the soft baby bunnies, and milked the cows. It was a beautiful experience where I once again felt the missing of George. We told the staff that four of us had been there almost thirty years prior, and they were awed that we had finally returned these many years later. Another circle closed.

# 22

## George's Basement
## . . . 1973 and Beyond

A MAGICAL UNDERGROUND PARK, a shelter for a mommy and her kittens, on special days transformed into a party with brightly colored balloons and a piñata—our basement was all things. For George it was a lure destined to be his sanctuary. He whiled away hours, perhaps years, in both reverie and toil in our basement. For him, the basement was the most remarkable characteristic of our lovely old home.

I cannot forget the day the real estate agent had pulled up in front of the pretty little house that was to become ours; he had called it "Tudor style," a catch phrase adopted by sellers. Although we had immediately liked the house, it was when the agent guided us down the stairs to the basement that George's eyes really lit up. To me, it was an ordinary basement, but to George, it was perfection.

The basement ran the entire length of the house, and George saw its potential. Turning left when you descended the steps from the kitchen, a dimly lighted wood-paneled room—complete with bar and gas fireplace—greeted you. Our girls never tired of playing around the bar, a neat space to create a pretend grocery store or a soda fountain where mommy served real drinks, or to find a great place during hide-and-seek behind the swinging door. All the kids in the neighborhood enjoyed that room, celebrating birthdays by pinning the tail on the donkey and eating cake. Later when the girls were older, the room sported a grand ping-pong table.

Thoughts of celebrations and child's play were not what drew George to the basement. It was the other side of the room, where the washer and dryer stood—rough-hewn wood and wide open—where George began his assault soon after we moved in. He outfitted that space with a massive worktable, complete with scary-looking tools such as great saws with giant teeth and a variety of huge hammers; a large vice stood staring, and thousands of different-sized nails and screws overflowed from dozens of boxes.

George decorated his side of the basement. He erected walls, built numerous compartments, installed his radio—often blaring out precious baseball games or *Mystery Theater*—and finally he hung pictures of his favorite baseball players. He was happy. The space was a work in progress, and where one day there was a wall, the next day would bring a new configuration.

George's basement was usually in disarray, but he could always find what he wanted. It was his workshop, his special place, with all manner of "thingamajigs" and strange pieces of this and that. If someone needed a special piece of metal or wood for a part or tool, he would say, "Hold on, I think I have something you can use," and down the stairs he'd fly to his place, and he would pull out the precise "thingamajig" that was needed—or if you were really special, he'd make a unique piece with his own hands.

For years, I hated his basement. I resented George's private escape, where he could quietly remove himself from the chaos taking place up those stairs—no kids, no homework, no problems. He was "working." Often he escaped from me, also escaping from interacting and from daily small intimacies. Later, after our years of therapy and the uncovering of the rich moments of our lives he had been missing when he holed up in the basement, things changed. It was still his place to think and reflect, but it no longer beckoned him the way it once had. He had joined us up that long flight of stairs.

# 23

## Our Daughter's Wedding
## . . . 1991/1992

GEORGE AND I WERE ON pins and needles, trying to suppress our excitement as we sat next to our daughter Christine, waiting for an elaborately planned surprise to begin. It was Christine's twenty-third birthday, and her boyfriend, Michael, who attended medical school in Iowa, wanted to surprise her at her dorm at New York University where she studied physical therapy. As part of the deception we had gone to her NYU dorm to wish her *Happy Birthday,* and found her alone and a little sad. As we conversed in one of the drab and empty common rooms, Michael appeared—"Surprise!"

Even more of a surprise was to come later on that memorable birthday, when Mike gave Christine a perfect sparkly diamond ring while they rode in a jolly hansom cab in New York's Central

Park that moonlit May evening. Michael is Jewish, so they set their wedding date for October 18, 1992—eighteen being a lucky number in the Jewish religion. An interfaith wedding was planned and both a priest and rabbi would celebrate the union of my daughter and my new son.

George removed himself from the details of the wedding plans, but he took his cherished daughter to see *Father of the Bride* so they could share some hilarious moments about this serious and beautiful event. Always a great kidder, he would rib Mike, "You still have time to jump into the car and make a clean getaway." Although he teased about being married, in secret he delighted in our relationship. But when I would ask, "Do you want to see a picture of Chrissi's dress, or my dress?" or, "Do you want to come with us to the reception hall and then to see the little apartment where they'll live?" he kept putting us off. He said, "I'll be surprised on the day of the wedding, and I'll see the apartment afterward." But that was not to be.

When George got sick, we were despondent. Preparations continued for Christine and Michael's wedding in October. We moved forward—but how? Even now, my brain screams when I think of anticipating the wedding with George in his "condition."

The stark whiteness of the rows of wedding dresses, with their glowing satin and delicate lace, contrasted sharply with the gloom of our predicament. Arriving for Chrissi's bridal dress fitting, I was shaken. She looked so beautiful in the lovely long white satin wedding dress that she would wear, her dark hair shining. But George would never walk her down the aisle. The tears flowed as the salespeople looked on helplessly. My mother-of- the-bride dress was a brilliant royal blue with tiny bugle beads at the hem. At the final fitting, alone in the dressing room, I sagged onto the chair, dissolving into tears. George would never see either of these enchanting dresses.

Although George's illness took some of the joy from the evolving plans, we somehow managed to live on two distinct planes of existence, with the wedding preparations continuing full steam ahead like a runaway train, and with all of us supporting each other through the harder times. The rehearsal dinner was excruciatingly heartrending for me. Josephine, my sister, came to hold my hand, and Mike's father cried. We were all thinking of George, even though no one mentioned that he was lying in a hospital, close to death.

Plans culminated on a stunning October day—almost one month after George had become sick—appearing to all as another picture-perfect, storybook wedding. I walked our daughter down the aisle, and cried throughout the ceremony, as the clergy prayed for Christine's sick dad as well as Michael's grandpa, who had recently died. Some guests were stunned by our plight, and probably wondered how we were so resolute. I, too, wondered. My brother, Bob—in George's place—escorted me into the reception room, but I had begged the bride and groom not to include the mother/son dance because George was not there to dance to "Daddy's Little Girl" with Chrissi, and they had graciously complied. I could not have suffered that. The video captured our family and friends talking, dancing, and crying, all keeping spirits as high as possible for Chrissi and Mike.

Our determination not to blemish the couple's long-dreamed-of day showed through in the smiling faces portrayed in the photographs taken beside the brilliant turquoise

Chrissi and Mike

swimming pool at the country club. Fall trees glowed with green, gold, and red leaves as they belied the melancholy. Amid flowers, music, and food, it was a spirited party in spite of the bittersweet flavor of the day.

Allowing myself a reprise, I did not visit the intensive care unit that day; the nightmare would wait for me as it lingered for yet another day.

George would not have wanted to spoil the wedding. Christine and Claudine planned, "When Dad is well, we'll get dressed again, and have a special celebration just for him." We dreamed of the day George would wake up from his coma, we would have a great party at our house, and all the friends and relatives who visited and nurtured us in the months following his operation would come—there would be a happy ending.

Chrissi and Mike went off on their honeymoon in Spain—what else could they do? We promised to keep in touch and take care of Daddy while they were gone.

I was in a daze, but I knew that if George had been with me, we would have gone to the young couple's apartment, and painted and helped with little details for the newlyweds' return. George would have dug right into those chores; he always did, and I wanted to do it for them in his absence. Finding some house painters in the *Pennysaver,* I forged ahead. Operating from a place of fear, I could not bring myself to trust these people. Trusting nothing, I felt that the world was no longer a safe place—but I wanted the tiny rooms to be painted for Chrissi and Mike, and the painters I found were cheap. Meeting them one morning at the apartment, I was in a crazed state, expecting them to run off with my puny two hundred dollars; they didn't. They painted rather poorly, but the apartment was clean. I accepted the outcome and moved on.

That was my life for the next year, and even after—divided into a world of heartbreak and tears contrasting with poignant flashes where the children in my life played, where our daughter, Claudine, started her new job as a teacher, and where a wedding took place. Again, the question: How could I survive? The answer: What choice did I have? I was alive, in spite of a crumbling reality—the reality of everyday life without George. Taking care of our dog and the cats, I got out of bed each morning with feet of lead as heavy as my heart. Being swept forward by the river of life, and marking off day after day on the calendar, I was carried along, sometimes on the brink of drowning.

# 24

## My Big Risk . . . 1992

WHEN GEORGE FELL ILL, we were just weeks from concluding a refinancing on our home. We had both worked diligently to complete the paperwork and finalize all the details. Now, George would not be able to sign papers at the closing.

In the panic-filled weeks following George's initial hospitalization, I made the brave decision to go through with the refinance. It had been our plan, and I was going to make it happen. Looking back at this incredible time, I have no idea how I had the courage to do what I did. The closing was scheduled, and I went to the meeting with Power of Attorney in hand. I was armed and ready to see this through. My friend Ruth encouragingly accompanied me for moral support, but we were on our own—symbolically—just George and me. I wondered how I could face those intimidating lawyers in their three-piece suits, along with their smartly dressed staffers seated at the long, cold shiny table piled efficiently with their folders.

The room felt freezing, and I entered alone. The story I had constructed was that George had been called to California, as his brother was gravely ill, and that he asked me to proceed with the closing as planned. They examined all the paperwork, passing it to each person involved. Believing they could tell I was putting up a false front, I shook inside, while showing only extreme calm on the outside. They signed papers, I signed papers, copies were made, more signatures were required; it seemed endless, and all the while I was expecting that I might be found out—but it was finally concluded.

I had proceeded without George, knowing he was "with me" on this—and my new mortgage was official. Whenever I think of what I did, I don't know where I found the strength. Little did I know I would need all the power I could muster and more, before George would be laid to final rest.

# 25

# Forgetting . . . 1993 and Beyond

I WAS SCARED; I WAS TERRIFIED of forgetting some cherished details about George. How his face looked up close, the scar on his neck, the way he smelled, his voice, his jokes, the safe way he made me feel. I wanted to keep every story about George, every anecdote and every joke he had told, close to my heart, but I could not, so I treasured the moments when someone reminded me of something he said, or imagined what he might have said.

"I have a surprise for you Claudy," George had said, as he handed over a bag of yummy chocolate candies. This is one of many sweet memories I was fearful of losing. George rarely told his girls how special they were, but he proved it loud and clear by his actions. One was the candy, and there were other ways. No matter what his young daughters asked of him, he would get it, do it, buy it, or make it, and they would have what they needed. From painting their tap dancing shoes for their recitals year after year, to supplying the unique items needed for their science projects, or playing a game of Twenty-One in the driveway, he was their dad, and they were his treasures.

Our side door opens onto a long shared driveway just a few short feet from the house next door. Through our facing kitchen windows, we could wave cheerfully to our neighbors. My best friend Connie used to live there, and after she moved, I had been heartbroken until we met Josephine and John and their three children—Diana, David, and Daniela—who moved into Connie's house. George had been delighted that he would have a pal— John—to meet on weekend mornings to just "shoot the breeze." Summer mornings sharing coffee with John and Josephine had been especially joyful, and Jo tells a story of George that I hold dear. One summer day as they shared a morning cup of coffee, she remarked to George, "I don't know where all my mugs have disappeared to—some of them are missing." George came to her door a few minutes later with four or five mugs in his hands. He had riffled through our cupboard and found the missing mugs, and brought them to her, saying, "Theresa has been pilfering your mugs—she's a mug thief." It's true that sometimes I took a mug of coffee home with me and often forgot to return it—I still do. Only George could have turned the incident into a humorous event, taking great pleasure in teasing me. What I missed about George most of all was the way he had kept us all laughing.

This family became my family, especially since George's

George with his precious Daniela

illness. Since the very night he was struck down, I believe he knew he was leaving me in good hands, because they have surely been my saviors. A loving Italian family, they share holidays with me that are special to us both. Christmas mornings, when I wake up to the shock of being without George, I am not alone. In the years since George has been missing from our lives, in the midst of the happy chaos of boxes and torn-open wrappings, this warm family shares a glass of wine with me, and we exchange little gifts. We have had great parties on the Fourth of July with our extended families, feasting and drinking and playing raucous games. We mark all the important events together—birthdays, christenings, graduations, and weddings. How could I—or my children—have survived without them? I do not know.

I cannot believe that almost twenty years have passed since

George disappeared from the driveway and from our lives. Diana, the oldest of Jo and John's children, is now a beautiful dark-haired, dark-eyed young lady; she is a friend, and a mother to the charming two-year-old Joanna. David and I share many hours together, talking about life and sharing breakfasts at the diner, remembering George. Daniela, their youngest, was always our special little girl. She was like a granddaughter to George, the only one he would have the chance to know. As a baby, she was drawn to our house, just across the driveway. Her parents would wrap her in a huge blanket and quickly pass her to us so she could visit our dog Reddy Boy. George adored these visits; Daniela was four when George was taken from us.

Even when George was hospitalized, Daniela and I spent many hours together. (She continued to visit my home, especially to see the animals.) Once, we were riding in the car and saw a police car and an ambulance passing. Daniela asked, "Who is in there?" "Is it a girl or a boy?" "Are they going to die?"

Daniela was adorable about remembering George. She often asked about him, inquiring, "What happened to George?" I tried to explain what happened and she tried to understand. Then she asked about his "spirit." "Where is it?" These are the hard questions for all of us.

On another occasion, she said, "I know George looks like he's sleeping, but I know he is not really sleeping, because you wake up when you're sleeping, and he can't wake up." She was perceptive, and asked, "I wonder where he really is?" She answered on her own, eventually stating, "George is in heaven; he's my guardian angel." I had to hold back the tears, because I was driving the car at the time.

David, Diana, and Daniela

She is now twenty-three years old, and a brilliant and gorgeous young lady and college graduate. George would be so proud of her.

## We Carry On . . .

D URING OUR YEAR OF WAITING, Christine intuitively acknowledged my anger when—after George had been hospitalized for some months—friends and relatives stopped talking about him and our strange situation. She understood how I felt, and sent me a copy of a "Dear Abby" column that talked about the illness or death of a loved one being likened to a great elephant in the middle of the room, an elephant that no one speaks of or acknowledges. This is a common complaint of those whose lives are touched by tragedy. Our family and friends made fewer visits to the nursing home. Who could blame them? I didn't want to go either. They didn't say it in so many words, but they wanted to run away from the situation. So did I. Some spoke of him no longer. What could they say to comfort me? I hung a copy of the column on my fridge, made copies of it, and actually sent it to some friends. I hoped they got the message.

I certainly learned a life lesson myself. Now, knowing what I know, being through what I have been through, I understand that I must say something to someone who is suffering. We need to just keep saying we're sorry for the pain being suffered. We need to say we care about or love that person, and offer whatever is needed to help. Perhaps there is something concrete to do, or perhaps what matters most is simply offering a shoulder to cry on.

# 26

# The Journal . . . 1992/1993

A S WE ENTERED THE controlled chaos of George's hospital room, the pretty book lying on the bedside table attracted every visitor. The journal had been lovingly presented to our family by our friend Connie. A dreamlike scene on its vibrant cover shows a serene lioness surrounded by a menagerie of exotic jungle animals.

The journal gave us a job—something specific we could accomplish as we stood awkwardly gazing at our George in this unspeakable condition. The practice of jotting down our thoughts soon became a sweet tradition, the musings taking on lives of their own. Every visitor—friend and family alike—recorded entries as diverse and precious as their own personalities. The journal contains fervent prayers for George's recovery, accounts of the current football season, and words simply expressing how his jokes were missed. Each entry is a love letter to George or me or the girls.

A record of the endless days, the journal became a dialogue where we shared life-changing events and everyday happenings. In it, we documented George's sleep/wake cycles, wrote exhaustive tales of his condition, and made meticulous accounts of the treatment he received daily.

The ritual evolved into two artful journals, priceless keepsakes whose touching words eventually helped inspire me to write about George and his odyssey.

Many journal entries moved us to tears, while others brought laughs. George's friend Bob told of his fishing trip, Connie wrote about the pets, and Chrissi about her new job. Her dad had often teased his daughter about her great career as a physical therapist, now working at a rehabilitation center in our area. He asked, "Are they looking for a janitor over there?" And his younger daughter, the teacher, wrote excitedly about her first job. He had been really thrilled about her career choice, because he worked for the Board of Education too, and was proud of her accomplishment. Michael, our son-in-law, recently graduated from medical school and embarking on his internships, tried to take care of George the best he could. He felt helpless in the face of the situation. George had been tickled pink that one of his daughters was marrying a doctor, and the other would marry a Wall Street broker. Delighted with his daughters and his life, it was a happy time from which he had been plucked in an instant.

What follows are but a few of the most memorable sentiments of the journal:

The opening is entry is a simple one from Connie:

*I read a chapter of George's Baseball Book to him, and told the nurse he needs a shave.*

*Miss you George,*
*Love, Connie*

From Steven, George's nephew:
*Uncle George was sleeping, but I still read him the Sports page, and one chapter in his book. I brought the last card of the Ted Williams series for him, and made a Yankees sign to hang on the wall.*

From Michael, our son-in-law:
*Hi Dad, you look good. I hope you don't mind that I brought my stethoscope with me today—just to take a listen—you sound like you need to get up to clear your throat, and spit up something gross. I think of you every day and miss talking to you. I hope you can hear everything we say and feel our touch. They're taking good of you and you're very strong. Chrissi and I are well and happily married. We're hoping you'll get up soon so we can take you and mom away. We love you.*

*Michael*

From Connie:
*Terri is doing great standing up for you—you'd be proud of the way she's fighting for you. Miss talking about our pets together.*

*Love, Connie*

From my sister Josephine:
*George, I pray for your recovery and love you. You are always in my thoughts.*

*Your sister in law, and*
*fellow traveler,*
*Josephine*

From Evelyn:
*Theresa showed me all the wonderful letters you received over the years from the Board of Education. I put them in order by date and am going to get a folder for them.*

*Love, Ev*

From Michael,
*Hi Dad, They're resting you on your ear again, so I fixed you and put your Yankee hat on you. I just pray your little synapses are healing. It was very warm today; I think they should move you outside and let the sun shine on your face.*

*Love, Michael*

From Claudine:
*Hi Dad, it's 4:20 and I just came from work. We have a four-day weekend. You look good. We just heard Neil Diamond on the radio.*

*Love you, Claudy*

More messages we treasure:

From Chrissi:
*Happy Thanksgiving, Daddy! I brought my rosary beads from Grandma Mary [George's mother] and they are in a place of honor, next to your Yankees cap.*

From Bobby, my brother:
*Thanks for reminding me that we are all precious to each other. We will all be waiting for more messages from you. If you can, come back to us; if not, we will understand you are busy doing something very important.*

From Steven:
*I just want to thank you for all the great times I had with you at*

*the ballgames. I want to thank God for you. I pray every night that one time soon you'll be better. I'm waiting. We have a lot to talk about.*

From Connie:
*George, we talked about you on Thanksgiving—you reminded us that life is precious and one must be true to oneself. You taught me that and if I make mistakes, I learn from them. Thanks for living next to me, and for caring for my kids, me, and the SNOW!"*

From Connie and Billy:
*I know that you hear us whether we talk to you here or in spirit. You are very busy on a spiritual level, and doing very important work for your own soul and for all of us. You have touched each one of us and in your quiet way, you changed our lives. We remember your kindness, your caring and your helpful ways. Don't feel alone. We are with you in spirit always. Spirit has no barriers. Keep the love that surrounds you with you as you continue your journey.*

From Janet and Ruben:
*We came to visit you and figured if you heard that Barry Bonds was offered $42 million, you would snap out of it. Today, I got Pete Scourer's autograph.*

From Barbara, my friend:
*We Feerys love you—you are walking with God. You know the whole picture now.*

From Paul, our future son-in-law:
*It seems the women have stopped yapping in your ear long enough for it to heal [he had a sore on his ear]. I greatly miss*

*the games of Twenty-One in the driveway and my favorite Trivial Pursuit partner.*

From me:
*To my darling George – I'm trying to be brave; it's hard. I need you to help me keep my spirits up, as you have done for so many years. I miss you so, but I hear you telling me things—things to help me through. I hear you encouraging me, and just being you. There's so much I want to share with you.*

From Chrissi and Mike:
*Dad, you jumped and opened your eyes when we touched you, and then we jumped! We had a baseball disagreement that we need you to settle. Hurry up and wake up!*

From Bob, my brother:
*Well, here it is a few weeks before Christmas and you are still busy. We feel that very soon you will give us a new sign. I marvel at your courage and know you are inspiring us to new ways of tenderness and love. If this was a part of your life's work, then you are successful beyond your wildest dreams. I am glad that you and I began to talk in a closer way these past few years. Be of good cheer and Merry Christmas.*

From me:
*My honey – I'm here shedding my tears on you, as usual. You know me—the champion crier—another June Allyson. I know how you love her. I miss all the funny things you say—boy, do I wish I could pick up the phone at work and hear your voice. I wish I had all those brief, but funny and teasing telephone conversations on tape, so I could relive them again. I never realized how precious that simple gift*

was. You are really creating quite a stir at the Board of Education Retirement System. They're not quite sure what to do with you, but you're getting plenty of attention. You would get such a kick out of it. Our girls are a great comfort to me. I hope you're not angry, because we are doing the best we can. I can't find the best words to tell you how much I care.

From Steven:
Hi, Uncle George. Came to read the sports page and wound up reading you the whole paper, even "Ann Landers" and "Dear Abby." I had a good time with you tonight. We got to talk a lot and I was able to share my feelings for you.

Bye, Buddy.

From Claudy
Hi, Dad. Chrissi, Mom, and I are here to visit. It is Christmas Eve. We are rushing around as usual. Everyone will be over tonight. We'll miss you!

Love always.

From George's niece Lynn:
I have been thinking of you mainly because you're ill, but also because I found the tennis racquet you gave me for my 10th birthday. Now my kids play with it. You were always so generous, but more so with your love and affection.

From Claudy:
Hi, Dad. Mom and I are here. It is Sunday and tomorrow we are going to Atlantic City for one night. We both need a little vacation. Wish you could come. You look very peaceful.

We miss you. Love.

From Jo and John;
*The holidays were very hard without you. We went in to see Terri and the kids on Christmas morning and I kept looking around for you. We all miss you very much. Diana dreams that you are home and o.k. I tell her to hold that dream. Daniela still asks for you and David told me he misses you. The guys are making sausage today and I had to cry because I kept thinking how much you would have enjoyed being with them. You know how Mario and John loved to joke with you. Try to come back to us—it's not the same without you.*

From me:
*We're praying that God gives you peace and light—no suffering—only the joy you deserve; perhaps you'll see St. Francis soon [the patron saint of animals]. He understands you. You're missed at home; there's an empty space here for you. Please give us signs of your wishes and thoughts somehow. You are loved.*

From George's brother Mike:
*George, they had a beautiful mass for you yesterday at St. John's University. All your wonderful friends were there. You are a lucky guy to have such good friends.*

From Connie:
*I came to hold your hand and receive the love you hold in your heart for me.*

From Ralph, who—each and every time he came—simply said:
*I love you, George.*

From Janet & Ruben:
*Sometimes it seems we need to see you more than you need us. We miss you very much. You would enjoy the fact that Wade Boggs and Don Mattingly are on the same team. You are in our conversations often and in our hearts always.*

From Evelyn:
*I'm here with Theresa and Claudy, and I will be spending the night at your house, as I've done many times lately, hoping to give some comfort to your family.* (Evelyn had brought a big, fluffy dog to George; it remained with him, under his arm, near his feet, always with him, as a reminder of George's love and devotion to animals.)

From Claudy:
*Happy Easter, Dad. We will all miss you, especially today.*
*Love.*

From Steven and George's brother, Dom:
*Happy Easter; we brought you a Yankee schedule so you will know when the games are on.*

And then the last entry in the first book . . . from Chrissi:

*I remember when we started this book. I thought we would never finish all the pages; I thought this can't possibly go on that long, but it has . . . Dad, we miss you and love you as much as ever. You are always in our thoughts.*
*Chrissi and Michael*

# 27

# There's Nothing More We Can Do . . . 1992

Here's nothing more we can do for George," declared the head of neurology at the hospital. The first months of his hospitalization were coming to a close—it was now November. We inquired about a rehabilitation facility and he answered, "That is not a viable option, as there is no hope for rehabilitation." Looming before us was the realization that there were no more choices and that time at the hospital was quickly running through our own personal hourglass.

One cruel day, hospital staff inserted a feeding tube into George's stomach. He had been weaned off the respirator and was breathing on his own. Now artificial nutrition entered his body through the tube in his stomach. He would live on. The cruelty was that this small triumph was a tribute to his great

131

physical strength and not a sign of impending recovery. His brain had been irrevocably damaged.

Splints had been attached to his hands and feet so they would not atrophy, but they did anyway. Physical therapy had been provided initially, but was soon abandoned because there had been no response or improvement.

To my amazement, we came to understand that there are steps taken in hospitals—when all scans cease, no new examinations are given and no new doctors are called on for their diagnosis, no administering of any but the most essential medicines are given—and things move along on an even keel. The patient has to go. You find out, incredibly, that the hospital's role is ended.

Requesting a meeting with the family, the social worker's task was to discuss "the next steps." I was livid. How dare she ask me, "What plans have you made?" and, "Where shall we make arrangements for George to go?" My response was, "Didn't *you* do this to him? Shouldn't *you* take care of him for the rest of his life?" They persisted: "Would you like to apply for Medicaid?" (After all, we did not have unlimited funds, and health plans do not pay for nursing homes.)

That's where George had to go—to a nursing home. George was a fifty-eight-year old man. Until a few short and yet endless months ago, he had been vital and handsome and his next stop was a nursing home; finally, this somber, demoralizing blow.

# 28

## Legal Recourse
## . . . 1992 and Beyond

WAS INTENSE. I WORKED, visited George, and just lived. Beneath these basics, I began to pursue legal recourse for the "incident" that had befallen George. Papers were gathered and lawyers consulted. My attempts to procure medical records, and find out exactly what happened on that fateful night, often led me to a proverbial brick wall. The truth never came to light completely, but I forged ahead. Reams of medical records were finally obtained. Almost a month sped by before the actual operation report could be obtained. "It is being dictated," was the stated excuse. Then "It is being typed," or "It isn't ready." It was this; it was that. These reports, written in their medical jargon, representing half a forest of trees, revealed nothing new. The bottom line was that George was in a vegetative state, and no decisive reason for that to have happened to him could be determined.

I had returned to work, resolutely performing my duties between the tears. Daily dealings with the Board of Education, and with the Retirement Board, and attempting to make sure George and I received all we were entitled to, was daunting. Through the maze of telephone calls and paperwork, the people I consulted with were incredulous; they could barely continue our conversations, and clearly wished to escape from this terrible story and get off the phone. Since our vigil had begun, we prayed for George, sang songs to him, and talked to him. Recordings of little Daniela, his favorite little friend next door, and of his dog barking, were enthusiastically brought to his bedside in hopes of awakening him back to our world.

Every medical avenue was pursued. George was seen by another top neurologist, who was known for his ability to bring a number of coma patients back to some degree of consciousness. He gave us no hope, and was one of several doctors to describe George as being in a vegetative state. His report included the following: "Unresponsive to verbal or to noxious stimuli of his extremities. He does not respond to threat, there is no detectable eye blink to this maneuver. There are no spontaneous or evoked movements. Impression: No realistic or reasonable hope for any further neurological improvement. Recommendations: There is nothing to add to this current regimen of supportive care. He will clearly need long-term placement."

It was in the midst of this chaos that I miraculously found a place for George. The veterans saved him.

134

# 29

## The Veterans Save Us
## . . . December 1992/1993

O N ONE OF HER DAILY calls to me at my office, my
sister Josephine suddenly remembered—while
the rest of us had not—that George was a veteran.
With George's brother Mike's influence, we were able to
secure a place for George at the Veterans' Home in St. Albans,
Queens.

Although I hated University Hospital, the prospect of
leaving was frightening. After months, it had become a safe
haven of sorts. Disappointingly, the hospital had never asked
me if George was a veteran. Social services, who wanted him
*out,* did not even suggest it as an option. Despite the fact that
all things at the hospital had moved at what seemed to us a
snail's pace, this transfer was done in a day, so quickly it made
my head spin, and my heart break.

The sinking feeling in the pit of my stomach when I met George at his new chamber in St. Albans was unforgettable. My sister and I cried when we arrived at this dimly lit, sparsely furnished facility. The Veterans' Home in St. Albans was surrounded by beautiful green lawns never to be noticed by its inhabitants. The corridors were wide, damp, and quiet; it was an ancient building and there was no air conditioning. The tiny and wrinkled veterans lying so silently under the white sheets appeared to be dead. The rooms were hushed and motionless except for the ugly flypapers hanging from the ceiling, swaying slightly. It was incredibly dreary and we hated to see George ensconced there, even though we quickly decorated his room with cards and wonderful wedding photos to soften the surroundings. Still, another layer of despair accompanied this new chapter. We knew nothing more would be done for George. He would exist here and we would exist to visit him, talk to him, touch him, and pray.

The Veterans' Administration doesn't have much money and they do the best they can. The Home at St. Albans took good care of George, but it broke my heart every time I visited. Nurses were kind, but they didn't seem to understand why I came and went in tears. Each of my almost-daily visits to this place was nightmarish. The gray walls needed painting, the bare light bulbs glared; it was depressing to be there.

I did gain some small solace from the tiny chapel I visited at the Home each day, and from the local veterans who visited their comrades there regularly. Many patients had no other visitors, as perhaps their families and friends were dead or had stopped visiting this place of no hope. I loved these devoted men who always remembered their abandoned friends from long-ago wars.

Yet, arriving daily, my steps became slower, my legs heavier, my heart sadder. Walking slowly from the car down the paths, noticing the ice or snow or rain, and eventually the green of spring reappearing, it always seemed unreal. I felt queasy; I couldn't bear the smell of illness, of ancient men and women sitting, slumping, crying out, and dying. George lay in a wing of the facility where everyone was eerily quiet, almost silent, and unlike a hospital, few visitors came for the sleeping clients. I wanted to run away, and on my way out, I fairly fled. "I'm sorry, George, you are not here in this place," I would almost scream. Grateful as I was for the VA's care, none of us could save George. I cried some more.

And so, the year dragged on.

# 30

## Bittersweet Journey . . . 1993

HE GREAT AIRLINER lifted off the runway with the usual whoosh and there I was up in the air, escaping from all the sadness and turmoil on the ground below. Yes, I was really flying off on a vacation, while George lay motionless in his hospital bed hovering between two worlds, and attached by the silver thread. I, too, sorrowfully hovered between two worlds. Visions of my grim world on the ground flooded back—the smells and sounds and the endless somber days spent at the hospital and nursing home watching George's eyes eerily but involuntarily move left to right and back again. In these moments, my mind's eye's pictures were being whooshed away in the rushing sounds of the aircraft's engines as it zoomed through the sunlit blue spring skies. There had been times I envisioned myself running away from my sad life and now, for a few short days, I was really escaping.

I had tried to bring fun back into my life while George lay in his sleeping state, and allowed myself treasured hours spent with children in the family, swinging them high into the air and frolicking in the swirling surf. These times never failed to lift my spirits. George had always said, "Your middle name should be fun," and I didn't want to disappoint. Then, I shopped. Shopping with my daughters as if we were ordinary people rushing around Macy's or enjoying the stores dressed up for Christmas always briefly elevated my mood.

George and I had planned to attend our son-in-law's graduation from medical school in Iowa in the spring of 1993. Our daughter was to marry a doctor and George had been delighted. We anticipated going to the graduation, remembering the numerous times George and I had deposited Christine at the airport in the past two years to visit Mike in Iowa. Now, agonized as I had been over my decision, I really wanted to go. Christine and Michael had been married seven months earlier, just a month after George became ill, during the stretch of Michael's clinical work that he carried out in New York. Now, Michael's graduation ceremony was to take place.

I left George in the hands of our daughter Claudine, as well as some good friends and relatives who promised to visit him—if not every day, almost every day. As I boarded the plane with a heavy heart and under a cloud, my unusual journey began.

The swell of pride I felt at the emotional graduation ceremony sprang from both George and me as the young men and women—and especially our new son-in-law—marched into the auditorium, long hours of study and hard work completed, and now planning enthusiastically for a glowing future ahead.

Our little group—Christine, Michael, Mike's dad, and I—planned to extend our vacation in order to explore a piece of this unknown-to-me part of our country, the Midwest. The drive along winding roads famous for their history—once inhabited by Native Americans, replete with spectacular sights, and topped off by a visit to Mt. Rushmore—took my breath away. I stared out the window as scenes of buffalo herds grazing peacefully rushed by; I cried for the distance between George and me, and the precious time he was missing with our children. I laughed for both of us as I marveled at the funny little prairie dogs peeking out at us from their tiny holes in the earth. I wished George were with me. Great tears fell as I read my book about grieving and widowhood, as we traveled the highways; I felt like a widow already. George was gone. The taste in my mouth was bittersweet, and from that I could not escape.

It was a wonderful break, though, and it was a pleasure to experience the historic Black Hills and the glowing carved rocks featuring famous presidents, walking the spectacular scenic hills, and taking dozens of pictures of Devil's Tower—drinking in sights we had only read about in books or seen in movies. Later, Christine said, "How could you say you enjoyed that trip to Mt. Rushmore and Wyoming? You were so sad and crying all the time." What Christine could not have understood was that I experienced two feelings at the same time. Yes, I cried, but the beautiful sights and thrilling scenes of the trip are indelibly printed in my mind and remembered in my heart. I experienced it all for George and me.

# 31

# I Visit Psychics . . . 1993

The modest house was unremarkable and looked like every other home sitting on the quiet block on the South Shore of Long Island. I was a *wreck* on the drive out on the Southern State Parkway, and my heart beat wildly. I was to meet with George Anderson (how weird that his name was George), a world-famous psychic and medium who had written several books. His book *We Don't Die* seemed like a lifeline to me at this emotional time: by now George had been in his sleeping state for several months, and I wanted to know where he was in that netherworld, so hidden from all of us standing day in and day out at his bedside.

How had I come to be speeding to this sought-after appointment with George Anderson, for which I would pay two hundred dollars for a one-hour session? My niece's husband,

Augie, had read Anderson's book, and was both enthusiastic and skeptical about its message. Augie's father had died young—in his fifties—and Augie desperately wanted to hear from him. He'd telephoned the number he was given, and spent days at the other end of a busy signal; finally his call had been answered and he was granted not one, but two appointments (his friend wanted a reading too). I knew of the plan and begged Augie to try magically to get me a slot too, even though I knew the protocol was for clients to arrange personally for their own readings. And it might take months for me to schedule a visit, because George Anderson was very much in demand.

Augie called me at work early on the morning of the appointment. He said, "Get a small tape recorder and be ready to leave at a moment's notice, because I don't think my friend is going; he's too nervous." At lunchtime, I secured the tape recorder, and waited anxiously.

Augie phoned again. "You're going with me, so get yourself together, and leave work immediately."

Both Augie and I were edgy. What would he tell us? We hardly spoke to each other on the trip out. We were afraid to break some magical or imagined spell.

Since George had become ill, slipping into his sleeping state, I'd begged the Universe for his life, although I had not been a practicing Catholic since I was a little girl. Everyone constantly spoke desperate prayers for George, brought back special holy water from Rome for George, said countless Masses especially for him, and made desperate pleas to the saints. There were those who embraced the sentiment, "There are miracles." I clung to their words, any words, and hoped that maybe indeed there were miracles. I couldn't know for sure. But on that day I believed it was a small miracle that had brought me out to Long Island, the more dramatic because Anderson didn't know that someone by the name of Theresa Cerrigone was coming to see him.

Augie went in first; I sat waiting in a small, simple, but comfortable anteroom. When Augie emerged, we did not speak. I stepped into the quiet, serene room with tape recorder in hand, and trembled. A diminutive, balding man sat before me with a large yellow pad and a pencil in his hand. All the while he spoke, his hand scribbled on the pad. This was automatic writing, and he seemed to be in a trance. Mr. Anderson revealed what he perceived to be the truth. He immediately told me, "There's a man standing beside you, young by today's standards."

I think I said, "My husband."

"He's on the other side," he replied.

I protested, "No, he's not." But Mr. Anderson insisted: "He's on the other side."

I finally had to tell him that George was in a coma, or vegetative state.

"Often people in that state come across as being on the other side," he said. His answers were somehow comforting.

He continued, "George is okay. He is gone, but still attached by a *silver thread*. He needs to be set free, and you can let him go . . . He loves you." And he added, "He has white roses in his hands, which signifies a wedding."

Of course, my daughter had been married a few short weeks after George got sick. Anderson said, "He was with you at your daughter's wedding. He is happy." He revealed that

George "was greeted as he crossed over to the other side by a little dog, happily barking and waiting for him."

George Anderson spoke—he referred to the lovely little dog we had lost as "she"—and I was convinced. George was gone. He spoke about my mother, and what he said about her rang true. Laying his hand on his chest, Anderson revealed that George's illness had begun with his heart. He spoke of other dead people making appearances, and it all seemed to make sense.

The tape now sits in a special box with other remembrances of George. It has been played for family and friends, and everyone has been dutifully inspired and surprised at the insights.

Later that year, I visited Glen Dove, another psychic and medium—a strange and extraordinary day. Stuck in congested traffic, and in tears, I arrived at Dove's home, believing I had missed my coveted appointment. When I knocked at his door, he welcomed me into his peaceful home and told me that his next client had canceled: I would have my reading. He was kind, and charged less money, and I came away with the strength to make some difficult decisions—decisions I had known I would have to make, but now made peace with.

The other evening I was sitting alone in a darkened movie theater watching the movie *Hereafter*. I was transported back to my time of bewilderment and hope, remembering my sentiments of so long ago—if only it were true, if only there was a hereafter when we would all meet again.

Playing the old tapes again several times over the years, I have not allowed myself to be bowled over by the words; I always conclude that people hear what they wish to hear. My final thoughts are always, "If George were on the other side, and could contact anyone, why wouldn't he contact me?" I believe he would!

### Wife, How Do I Love Thee?

It's our 11<sup>th</sup> year, of which I boast,
For you my love, I give this toast,

In our decade plus one, we've shared a life
That's had its joys, and sometimes strife.

We've had our ups; we've had our downs,
We've had our tears, we've laughed like clowns,

So again, I toast with love so true,
Cause all that I want is to be with you.

Love always and after that,
George

# 32

## Automotive Says Goodbye: George Remembered and Retired . . . June 1993

B ROOKLYN AUTOMOTIVE HIGH SCHOOL stood im-
posingly before us, reminding me bittersweetly of how
George had come to love this little neighborhood bor-
dering Williamsburg and Greenpoint. Greenpoint—with its
neatly scrubbed houses, the tiny Mom and Pop stores, and its
Polish influence in the charming, inexpensive little restaurant
George delightedly found—was magical. Automotive, as we
affectionately called his school, was a familiar place where
George once sneaked our teenage girls up to the rooftop on a
July Fourth night, so they could view the spectacular Macy's
fireworks from the best vantage point, proving that he was
"cool."

Now, years later, we were back at Automotive on this day
in June 1993. George was a machinist at this high school, the

only one in New York City where young men and women could actually learn to take a car apart and put it back together. He delighted in helping the kids, and was saddened when he saw some of them abandoned because of poor teachers, uninterested parents, or because they had special needs. When Automotive participated with schools from other cities in a competition to put an actual car together in the fastest time, he was so proud when they came in first or second, as they often did.

It had been nine months since George entered these golden doors, and we could hardly grasp that he still lay in his "resting vegetative state," while we, his family, had been invited to attend the annual awards ceremony where—this year—George would be remembered.

George's brother Mike, my friend Connie, my daughters, and I shakily ascended the steps at the ancient high school where George had spent many bright days in the past twenty years. How would it feel to walk the same steps that our George had trodden these many years?

This stunning building might have been old, but the corridors shone with worn tile and gleaming wood; artwork and pictures of dignitaries special to this venerable institution lined the walls. Led to seats of honor in the auditorium, through our tears we allowed the touching words recognizing George for his fine career and cheery personality to be a balm for our sadness. We gathered close together as school friends remembered him; an emotional tribute followed, and it was clear that George was a favorite to many in the cavernous room. "Your good nature and warm smile will be missed by all," the plaque lovingly presented to us reads; it hangs in our living room.

What cannot be forgotten are the tears and sadness apparent in that great auditorium; the words of love and affection echoed for him, and the obvious void felt by his friends: the teachers, the secretaries, the paraprofessionals, and his favorites—the lunch ladies, on that day in June. The following year, George was further memorialized in Automotive's yearbook for his charm, generosity, and good humor.

The marking of this celebratory tribute was but a stop on the speeding train toward the day when I would have to separate George, via retirement, from the Board of Education; he was alive, but running out of sick and vacation days.

My path was clear: get all we were entitled to. Try maneuvering any health and welfare system, especially a huge entity like the New York City Board of Education—it's punishing. Plunged, somehow, into insensibility on some level, and yet tending to the mundane issues bombarding me daily, I call personnel, leave messages, find the right department—leave messages, call the union, leave messages. Who would help us? Who could ensure George's rights and money? I simply couldn't lose all he had worked so hard for; he would have been so disappointed in me. Sequencing the steps through bureaucracy was fraught with twists and turns. Meticulously, my voice tight, I explained to countless numbers of faceless people on the other end of the line the somber tragedy that had happened. Sometimes those people were kind and caring, sometimes they seemed uninterested—perhaps they were uncomfortable. Most were horrified when I related his plight. They wanted to help me or they just wanted to get rid of me—either way, I was undaunted.

George had rarely been absent from work prior to this illness, so he had accumulated hundreds of sick days and had been on payroll for months. I surmised that George would have to retire after all the sick and vacation days were used. So I took step after painful step planning for that eventuality, even though on some days I could barely pick up the grey telephone; it felt heavy in my hand, like life itself. Then the secretarial training kicked in, as I locked my eyes on the all-important "things to do" list and carried on muddling through the mire, often in the midst of tears. As my colleagues watched my frenzied activities and teary breakdowns, they tiptoed around me each day; I was inconsolable in the months following George's descent into a deep coma, inconsolable, numb, and in fight-or-flight mode, too. Those same colleagues who tiptoed around my desk each day were incredibly kind and supportive. Brightly colored flowers from Diane's garden appeared daily on my desk and she brought me yummy food to brighten a devastating day. Cheryl listened to my interminable woes, and my friends were saddened for me and for George. He had managed to win their affection just days before becoming ill, when he arrived at our new office space, turning on the charm and helping everyone to settle in, hanging bulletin boards, and generally being the "nice guy" that he was.

Now, the months ebbed by and, incredibly, June was approaching; time was running out.

Barely hearing the technical words spoken, I—along with my sister, Jo—began our meetings with the Board of Education Retirement System. Each meeting was difficult and painful. Understanding our rights was a grueling task, and comprehending the choices and the rules was challenging. Once again, though bewildered, I made the best decisions I could. With advice from friends, family, and experts, the deed was done. George was officially retired from the Board of Education, and those long-sought retirement checks miraculously began to arrive in the mail. Miserably, George could not share in the joy of retirement. He never would.

# 33

## The Court Case
## ... Early 1993 Through Jan 2000

CAUGHT A GLIMPSE OF my anxious face in the reflective bronze finish on the elevator doors. I was struck by the golden opulence. My little "French heels" sunk into the plush green carpeting. It was inches thick, and my feet silently crossed the huge, richly paneled room. I was uncomfortable; my clothes weren't smart enough. I was intimidated but my pain emboldened me.

Dark wood paneling, stunning artwork, and lush plants made me slightly dizzy as I entered the law offices of P and W. I had painstakingly gathered up the reams of paper collected as a result of stalking hospital clerks, alternately begging, pleading, and demanding the complete and truthful records of George's days at University Hospital. These indecipherable hospital records told the story—a story without words, with only the same unchanged ending. George was gone, never to return.

Today I was armed with the facts and ready to do battle and plead the case that George had been harmed by the very people who had vowed to help him: the doctors and the hospital personnel. I had been informed when I telephoned prior to this appointment that they "would take the case." They knew harm had been done. Quietly I placed the heavy envelope on the pleasant law assistant's desk, and in January 1993, legal proceedings against the hospital and doctors related to George's case began. I knew these proceedings would drag on for years, so I left the offices and went on with my life, working, taking care of my pets, and stumbling through my grief.

Within a month I was summoned by serious young attorneys to sit at their long, shiny table where a court reporter would record my deposition of all matters relating to the case. These proceedings were chilling. I told myself that there was nothing to fear because truth was on my side. These were my lawyers and they were not menacing. I told the story as I have told it here—how one day George was a vibrant, laughing man and the next day he was forever lost to us, his mind damaged beyond repair, now in a netherworld about which we could only imagine.

Pages of depositions were collected at those very offices, given by the various doctors and nurses involved with George's illness. How eager I was to hear their story of what happened to George in their own voices. Regretfully, those answers and depositions were closed to me. I had wished I could have run up to the surgeon and grabbed his jacket to shout at him and plead, "What happened?" But as I remembered the days just after the tragedy, as they had passed me in hospital corridors, never speaking to me, and barely looking my way, I finally surrendered and acted like the sane woman I was, hardly recognizing the crazy woman I felt like in my head and heart.

There was little communication with my busy, somewhat intimidating attorneys until seven long years later; seven years of working, planning another wedding, and changing jobs. Each day of those years, I had lived with sadness and grief alongside a good measure of joy and happiness. Finally, the call I had been waiting for: the attorneys wanted to talk to me about money. I had thought about the money. I pictured and wanted millions; that's what George was worth to me. Sadly, I was informed that New York State doesn't award millions. Yes, they sort of laughed when I said "millions."

Once more, I crossed the shiny threshold of the offices of P and W.

In this seventh year, I rejected the first offer, which our attorneys had offered me on behalf of the hospital. Some weeks later, they came back with a second offer, practically doubling the first. My powerful but forgettable attorney nudged me toward acceptance of the offer advising me that "you never know about the outcome of a jury trial," and so with the support of my daughters, it was decided we could accept the monetary offer on the table.

The offer of money was literally on the table at the even-more-gorgeous office than I had been to on my first appointment seven years before. It was the office of one of the partners (partners usually "close the deal") of the firm, where I now sat flanked by my sons-in-law. Of course, as I shakily signed multiple copies of legal papers, I was declaring my agreement that neither the hospital nor the doctors had admitted any blame for what happened to George. It is a stipulation of the settlement—that no blame is assumed as a result of their payment of monies in the lawsuit—a bitter pill to swallow. Queasiness settled in my stomach when I signed the papers, because they *were* to blame for George's condition. No money could make up for the loss of George's life, of course, but the settlement has helped me, and our children, to live more comfortably. Each and every time we use the money, we say, "Thank you, George!" or "Thank you, Daddy."

# 34

# Send Me No Flowers . . . 1967

N O GORGEOUS BOUQUET of red or yellow roses stood on the windowsill; no small flowering plant, nosegay or even a bunch of mixed flowers bought from a street vendor graced my room. Having just given birth to my first child, a little wrinkled pink daughter, I was happy and scared. Sure, I noticed the other brilliant bouquets presented to the new mothers in the other rooms and a pang of disappointment clouded the joy. "It's Mother's Day weekend, Theresa," George said as he approached me empty handed. "It's a rip-off," he added. Instead of flowers, a card with a poem George had written greeted me when I arrived home. Consumed with mothering and all the fears and happiness accompanying a new baby in the house, I was not aware of my feelings. In fact, looking back, I never examined my feelings—

it was go forward, live, do, keep the household afloat, or be angry and fight.

The same bouquet-less scene was repeated three years later at the birth of my second daughter, who looked like a tiny prizefighter and her Uncle Joe when she emerged. "It's Easter," George said, "another rip-off." And yes, a poem greeted me at home.

### To the Happy New Mother

To our favorite person,
From us your family crew,

We wish to say we love you,
And hope these words will do.

To one whose heart will guide us
Through all our daily strife,

Whose devotion, strength and patience,
Gives deep meaning to our faith in life.

Love,
Christine, Thumper, and Me

George had surprised me with an exquisite pear-shaped diamond ring when he asked me to marry him on Valentine's Day at the Fifth Avenue hotel in Manhattan years before the babies were born. That was special. Early in our marriage, various gold charms followed: a tiny record engraved with the words "Try to Remember," our wedding song; a Merry Christmas charm with tiny colorful chips; a little golden ship celebrating his forever joke of how I'd caught the boat when I married him, and a baby carriage charm to remember the birth of Christine, our first daughter. Claudine, our second daughter, never got a charm. By then, that's how life was heading. There were endless bills, we were saving to buy a house, and there was never quite enough money. Shortly after we married, George informed me that he was selling his share of the tool and die business in which he was a partner. Why didn't I get angry when I heard that news? I should have—but I was numb during those years. I stayed home with the girls, and only went back to work when they were in school. We drove old clunker cars, and never decorated an entire room from top to bottom. If we needed a couch, we bought a couch, or a washing machine, or a lamp. Our babies had everything and I never failed to shop; plastic credit cards saw us through. But there were no flowers, and no more gold jewelry.

Envious of my friends who received bouquets of flowers delivered for Valentine's Day or birthdays, I was silently sad; twinges of jealousy also surfaced when friends received sparkling gold jewelry.

George always spent money on maintaining our home, but it was never anything I could see; it was shooting insulation into the walls, after which I cried when I saw the holes remaining that needed to be plastered. No flowers or candy for Valentine's Day. He said, "Neither one of us needs chocolates, do we?" More sweet poems found me.

## To Our Valentine

Mommy, Sam, and I would like to say: the best to you
   in every way,

We wish we could bring gifts of worth, to one whose
love is ours to take.

You do so much to bring us joy; each day begins with
fun and toys.
We hope we're worthy of all you did, for Sam and Me,
the Rotten Kid.
~St. Valentine's Day, February 14, 1969

I was over fifty when my first huge bouquet of flowers
arrived—from my son-in-law Mike. He sent me fifty-two
carnations when he was in medical school in Iowa. With
George in the hospital, the more than two dozen pink blossoms
lifted my spirits.

My daughters have sent me flowers, and my friend Tom
sent flowers for my birthday, but these gifts could not compare
to flowers that George might have sent me. Even though he
wrote me countless numbers of little poems that I love, he
should have splurged and bought me the flowers and gold
trinkets I longed for. Once he surprised me on Christmas
morning when I was greeted by a shiny brand-new blue bike.
I cried and was incredibly touched. But I don't have my
sparkling diamond anymore because it popped out of its precarious setting when I was riding my new bike to the park with
my kids.

In more recent years, I've spent plenty; I've been able to
help with down payments for my daughters' homes, have had
brand new windows installed in the house, remodeled the
kitchen, provided endless fun and games for all our grandchildren, and I've been able to travel. Of course, there is more

money now because of the lawsuit settlement. I had to lose George in order to more than "make do." I would have gladly signed on to "make do" for the rest of our lives if I could have only had George with me.

Two holiday poems from George:

### At Easter

On Easter Day, I say to you,
With love so deep and oh so true,
When others choose to show this day,
Their fancy clothes and hats so gay.
But, my love, in rags or lace,
You're the tops around this place.

### Christmas Again

It's Christmas again,
And we express our best
To our favorite person,
Who brightens our nest.

We give this gift to you,
Its value does not become,

We hope this blanket will do,
When years make you old,

It will help you survive the winter nights,
When Daddy's feet grow cold

~Christy, Claudy, June, Sam,
and Our Guest Pickles, and a Friend

# 35

## Another Doctor . . . 2011

THIS DREAM IS UNLIKE many, many dreams I had in the early years where George appeared and is not dead. I used to wake up and actually believe he had not died . . . I could not separate reality from the dream for a few moments until I became fully awake.

*I'm frantically calling a telephone number that I can barely make out on a card someone has given me. I struggle to make out the number, always getting one of the digits wrong as I dial. It's so frustrating. My friends tell me George called and he's okay; he's not dead. I don't believe them. He has died in the war. I convince them that he's gone, and I continue on alone again.*

The dream awakened me, and I began to think of another chapter for this book: my encounter with the doctor who was cruel to me at the Veterans' Home so many years ago. It saddens me that I couldn't get mad at him, I couldn't tell him off; I wish I had, but it's too late now—it's almost twenty years later, and he's probably dead, too. So I go to the computer, annoyed that it's turned off. Determined to get this down, I turn it on and type.

In 1993, I wanted to give George every single chance to come back to this world from his balancing act; he breathed, his eyes randomly rolled from left to right, he choked on his saliva as it caught in the vent in his neck, but we had been convinced that he felt and knew nothing. As he was living in his netherworld, so I was teetering in my own world. After months of trekking the long dreary hallways of the Veterans' Home in St. Albans, I decided to consult one more doctor before making the final decision to remove George's feeding tube. This time, it was the physician at the nursing facility. There's no doubt about it, I want confirmation that George can not, will not, come back from his somewhere-land.

I made an appointment and arrived at the expected time. I was alone. Foolish of me, not to have support—a friend, a daughter—but no, I am alone. The doctor is unremarkable, and I'm not sure—because I couldn't tell until he began to speak— if he is kind or unsympathetic. I retell for the hundredth time "The Story of George." I supposed he might know George's case—after all, George is listed as one of his patients on the ward, but I didn't ask whether he knew George at all, I just forged ahead with the story. When I finished, all he had to offer when I told him I was planning to have the feeding tube removed was, "Well, you're not paying for his care here, are you?"

I was crushed. I took his comment to mean that since I wasn't paying for his care, I should let him remain in the vegetative state, let him stay here to rot, continue to mourn him as I came to visit every other day now—his tone and his remark were accusatory. It was clear that the doctor did not consider why I might want to put George and ourselves out of misery. I wanted to run out of the doctor's office, and I did so as soon as I could. If only I had been stronger at the time, I could have defended myself and my plan; but no, all I felt was that my plan had not been acknowledged or approved of. This nobody, this bureaucrat of a physician, had managed to crush me, even though the Ethics Committee of the facility, my family, George's family, and all our friends supported me in my decision; this one, lone dissenting voice crushed me and it took me time to recover.

Soon, for survival's sake, I pushed the incident with this doctor from my consciousness, and rarely let it surface, except for this little piece of the story. I suppose the experience was quite significant to me because I obviously have not forgotten it, and I have chosen to include this hurt along with all the other cruelties suffered within George's sad story. So here it is, another punctuation mark, another emotional nail put to paper, and perhaps by putting it on paper, the anger, pain, and questioning will end here.

# 36

## The End of Waiting . . . 1993

OR ME, GEORGE HAD DIED that day in September 1992. So when, one day, George's brother said, "Why don't we put George in a wheelchair, and take him out into the outdoor area, and have a sort of picnic?" I was horrified.

I said, "No!" I was preparing to let George die.

My resolve was reinforced by imagining a most amazing funeral for George. The details emerged in my head as I trudged to the nursing home. Before that funeral was to become reality, though, I would need to muster supreme strength and I was moving toward it full steam ahead.

There were fears and moments of unbelieving as to how this would play out, but George's fate had taken on a life of its own and the hours were zooming toward the inevitable.

It was September 1993, and the one-year mark of George's persistent vegetative state approached. While George's condition remained constant—he still lay motionless in that high bed, under the white sheet, in that dimly lighted room, looking strangely handsome as though sleeping—I awoke one morning knowing it was to be a different day than all the nearly 365 days that gone before. This was the day I would request that the last machine keeping George alive be removed.

This choice had ultimately been made by me alone, after these twelve months of soul searching. My stomach was nervous as my morning routine proceeded deliberately: let the dog out, feed the cats, take a hot shower, and get dressed. How should I dress for this occasion? Is it important to look nice, to look as though I am in my right mind? Is it important to look attractive—will they notice or care? I gathered the papers locked in the old, battered strongbox, and as though in a dream—as every meeting with hospital personnel, lawyers, and social workers seemed—I was on my way to my appointment with the bioethical panel of the Veterans' facility. My brother, Bobby, George's brother Mike, and our dear Connie found ourselves once again enveloped in a crisp and sundrenched fall day. What a day to end life; there was a desperate irony in the air, as we made our way to St. Albans in Queens. Feeling small and insignificant, I alone was ushered into a large, ancient, and sparsely decorated room at the Veterans' facility. Three panel members greeted me without warmth. I thought I might need to plead my case for George to be allowed to die, but they sat silently with impassive expressions on their faces. Not being able to read their looks, I handed them the papers. Speaking solemnly of my resolve to remove the feeding tube that artificially forced nutrition through all the now-still organs of George's beautiful body, I left the hospital to await their verdict. I was armed with the power of knowledge, because I had investigated the procedure of removing a feeding tube, and had spoken personally to families who shared their experiences in allowing loved ones to die with dignity. These families had endured the wrath of strangers in the public arena. I was fortunate and had not endured antagonism; mine was a private hell.

Feeling scared, as I left the Home on the familiar path, I knew an ultimate and irrevocable step had been taken. My steps were somehow lighter as I watched my feet rush along the path, as I glanced at my reflection in the familiar windows. Soon, I hoped, I would never again take this path. Still my heart was heavy, but I consoled myself: George will finally be free. Here I was, though—residing in two worlds: the ordinary world of eating, celebrating, talking, and sharing—and the other dark world where I was in an odd limbo waiting for George to die. It felt so curious, weird beyond words; why should I exist normally in the sunshine, when the world was upside down?

Almost a year before that extraordinary day in September, my friend had been wearing a marquisette butterfly pin— sparkly spun silver threads with a small garnet stone for its body. I had admired it. She had taken it off her jacket, and said, "It's yours." That pin was a treasure, but during that year I had lost it. Searching everywhere, I was heartsick, for it was nowhere to be found. Somehow it signified to me all that had been lost.

On that day in September 1993, I left George with the veterans and drove slowly home in my melancholy mood. When I arrived at my house, something glinted in the bright sun on the dashboard, in a corner not easily seen. There it was—the illusive and beautiful butterfly. It was my sign that George would soon be free. Each time a vibrant and richly colored butterfly floats by, my thoughts run to George and that day.

I needn't have worried about the VA's decision, because within twenty-four hours, the bioethical panel agreed with me, ordering the feeding tube to be removed and allowing George the chance to die with the dignity left to him and to us.

With the decision, I became calm, and apprehensive, too. Would it all go as planned? Would I suddenly panic and have regrets? What had I done? I read everything I could about what would happen to George as he left this world for good. My lifeline was the young woman who had watched her young husband die when his feeding tube was removed. She lived nearby and I called her often. She told me of the hospital fiasco that had left her twenty-nine-year-old husband in a vegetative state. Without a Living Will, she had to petition the courts to allow her husband to die. Many right-to-die cases wind up in court, with strangers making personal decisions for families. And then sometimes life support is simply removed, quietly, as long as the family is in agreement, and when there is no hope for a viable life. The hospital did ask me early on if I wished life support to be removed. But at that time it seemed too early; I couldn't say goodbye after only a month, when all those expressionless doctors were still saying, "George could awaken at any moment." No, I had needed time to think.

Now, recalling that emotional time when George lay peacefully as we waited for his breathing to cease, I realize that even with my doubtfulness, I never really had second thoughts. In fact, when I remember George in "that condition," I think, *Yes, yes, I made the only decision that could have been made.* The young woman whose husband had been allowed to die told me it had been quiet, peaceful. In our many conversations, I clung to her comforting words, as she guided me in detail through the hours and then days she and her husband's mother stood at his bedside waiting for the end. As we talked, I droned on about my vacillating thoughts. She said, "Stop! The bioethical panel would not have so quickly and readily agreed, if they had any doubt about George's condition." They understood, she understood, and I understood—it was right.

All the while, the courageous veterans came to George's bedside to say a prayer and lay a comforting touch on his arm, and for that I am forever grateful.

It would take approximately two weeks for George to die after the feeding tube was removed. Our family and friends never questioned me. They were grateful and kind enough never to be more than comforting. They wanted neither George's suffering nor ours to go on. Not knowing if he was suffering physically, we believed his soul was anguished, still attached to this world, but just holding on by a long silver thread to the other side. We believed his soul was tortured, as were ours.

The deathwatch was quiet and peaceful, and some days passed. There was no unpleasantness, and we continued to visit daily. George's breathing became shallow, and in fact, it was more peaceful than usual; no tubes, no suctioning his throat, just silence and peace.

George died on September 25, 1993—twenty-one years to the day after our baby's life had been saved. Gratefully, Chrissi and Mike were visiting at the nursing home on that Saturday morning and were with him when he stopped breathing. They frantically called me and I rushed to the Home with George's brother Mike, not quite believing it was finally over. I was aware of my every deliberate move and my shallow breathing. Wishing to savor these moments, as I knew they could never be reprised, I said my final farewell and kissed his face and hands for the last time. He still looked as though he were sleeping.

The journal entries written at the end of the year in which George remained in his long sleep were especially beautiful and painful, as each of us said goodbye to him in our own special ways. He certainly inspired us all to write, and reach deep down into our hearts to communicate what we were feeling.

And the last entry in the journal from Michael:

*Goodbye Dad. Peace, Be Still.*

*Love,*
*Chrissi and Mike*
*September 25, 1993*

*The traveler must be born again on the road, and earn a passport from the elements. (Thoreau)*
And so, I have had to be born again.

# 37

## The Funeral . . . September 1993

I AM AN OBEDIENT WOMAN, obeying traffic regulations and paying taxes on time. I am law abiding and was a faithful wife and a responsible mom. When it came to George's funeral, however, all bets were off. I vowed to honor him with a tribute from my heart to his, having had the better part of a year to plan it, as he lay in his sleeping cocoon. Throwing caution to the wind, obedience to tradition and church was abandoned.

Friends and family tiptoed around me, allowing me to survive this challenge in my own way. It was to be no ordinary funeral—and if we can conceive of a funeral as extraordinary, George's was. The final tribute to George had to be unique, honest and worthy of this special man.

The coffin was of wood—there would be no mahogany,

cherry or even steel. (George had treasured wood and hoarded as much as he could, as witnessed when the garage was finally torn apart for a clean-out. He might have built a small house with it.) It was a simple, inexpensive, but attractive casket, because we heard George's voice whispering in our minds, "Are you crazy? It's too much money . . . No—still too much money," and so it was as he would have commanded. He wore no conservative blue suit, nor any tie, and definitely no shoes. (George took his shoes off as soon as entered our home each evening.) His beloved Yankee jacket, its satiny blue gleaming against the white velvet casket interior, accompanied him to the beyond. He never wore it in life, but it was his shroud in death.

The sanctuary where we said goodbye to George was a handsome and familiar old white clapboard house in our neighborhood. As we entered the great double doors, we stepped slowly and noiselessly on the thick carpeting while strains of Neil Diamond's "Sweet Caroline" greeted us. It was the music I had insisted upon—so special to us. Neil's music continued to serenade us as we gathered to pay our last respects and send our love to George on his journey.

The solemn room and first glimpse of George brought tears of joy and sadness. George, extraordinarily handsome, looked as though he were sleeping peacefully as he lay in the glowing blue satin Yankee jacket.

During the weeks and months of his long slumber, a written tribute had been forming in my mind. This became a remembrance booklet commemorating George's life, given to all who visited us during the viewing and funeral. It included several poems by George, a short biography, and the moving hymn "On Eagles' Wings." The booklet conveyed our family's gratitude to all who offered prayers, love, and food, as the endless parade of desolate days and bleak nights took over our world.

September 1992

The picture of George looking out at us from the last page of the booklet captured him in his plaid flannel shirt leaning on boxes of presents in our driveway. It had been taken on the day of our Christine's bridal shower, a few short weeks before he got sick. It was the last photo ever taken of George and one in which he looked so handsome—dark haired with just a trace of salt-and-pepper strands, with his familiar five o'clock

177

shadow caressing his face. I now refer to that shot as "the picture of Dorian Grey," because George grows no older than on that wonderful sunny day. Copies of this photograph grace refrigerators and mantles of many of those who loved him. It reminds us that George had not been able to walk either of his daughters down the aisle and that I had been robbed of the dream I had had for them since they were babies. In place of the fulfillment of that dream, in addition to our tribute for the funeral, were words sung by George's favorite performer, Neil Diamond, which dignified the back cover of the booklet. These words were comforting, the refrain teaming lyrics from the movie *E.T.* with Neil Diamond who wrote and recorded the popular song.

*"Turn on your Heart light . . .*
*Let it shine wherever you go,*
*I'll be right there . . ."*

George's funeral was as touching a tribute as any funeral ever. Planning the minute details was therapy for me and for my friend Connie, too. Ah, Connie—what can I say about my friend? She had been with me from the very first night George got sick until the end—or the beginning of George's transition and spiritual journey, however we want to look at it.

We had no attachment to the Catholic Church, so the service took place at the funeral home. Precious photographs of our family kept George company when we went home for the night. Dozens of flower arrangements were sent even though we had asked that donations be made to the Doris Day Animal League in lieu of the glorious blossoms we received anyway. Not everyone knew of George's habit of jotting down little ditties for us, or of his long poetic offerings on baseball or animals. Lying quietly on the table near his earthly body was George's touching book of poems for all to enjoy and to see a glimpse of the "inner" man.

Our Unity Pastor, Pat Filliout, looked like an angel as she spoke the solemn words of the culminating ceremony. Pat was dressed in a flowing white robe, and soft piano music accompanied her as she sang hymns in her clear and lovely voice—and as she remarked at how George had been "a blessing to others' lives." Among the comforting words she chose was a reading of the wonderful "The Traveler," by James Dillet Freeman, a Unity poet laureate.

Most inspiring and touching, though, were the eulogies by my friend Connie Levin, and Connie's son, Christopher Paoloni, now a young man, who grew up just across the driveway from George and me, along with his little sister Melissa, who hadn't even been born when we moved next door to their family. Then there was George's nephew Steven Cerrigone, who had stood beside his uncle's bedside for an entire year . . . and then came the hymns and songs performed brilliantly by our friends Judy and Joe Gagliano's son, Joseph Gagliano, Jr.

It has been almost twenty years, and I have now decided to listen to the audiotape made on the day of the funeral. I'm not sure why I have waited so long to listen, but somehow the time has come. The tape has rested in the memory box, with all the other mementos from that day, and I feel trepidation as I take it in my hand. What am I afraid of? The sadness? The tears?

I am taken back and taken aback at the clarity and beauty of the tape. I am transported to the dignity and sadness of the day. Yes, of course, the tears have come—many tears, once again—but poignant gratitude has once again given me peace.

I am forever thankful to Joe Gagliano for his glorious rendition of "On Eagles' Wings." I can envision George being lifted up, as we were all lifted up that day—with Joe singing so sweetly and asking us to sing with him if we knew the song; I could hear, ever so softly, Connie's voice in the background.

Connie, Steven, and Chris spoke of their relationships with, and their memories of, a man named George, and Joe thrilled us with his music. George's caring for all of us, his love of animals and baseball, and his down-to-earth genuine humanity came through loud and clear. I was grateful for their willingness to speak about George and for the honesty with which they spoke. Steven's words:

*I was asked to say a few words this morning for George Cerrigone—my uncle George—but when I sat down to write, I didn't know where to start; there are so many good things to say about a man who has done so much for family, friends, animals.*

*George was a husband, a father, an uncle, and most of all, a friend. He was loving and caring—a serious man, but with a great sense of humor. He has touched so many people in so many ways, as we have seen by the respect you have shown him this past year and especially in these last couple of days. He was the type of person everyone loved. He was there when someone needed him; he never turned anyone away. When called upon to do a task—whether large or small—he was there to help with no complaints.*

*He enjoyed work and took great satisfaction from it. But, I feel he most loved helping animals. They were something special. I remember him feeding the stray dogs, and he would say, "I wish I could take them all home and give them the care* they deserve." He knew that wasn't possible, but he was always there for them.

Uncle George meant a lot of things to all of us, and we all have our memories. I remember when we were kids—on Sunday morning at Grandma's house, we would play with him, putting on wigs, strumming on tennis rackets and singing into his old reel-to-reel recorder pretending to be The Beatles, singing 'I want to hold your nose . . .'—he was so much fun. I used to call him Uncle Sloppy 'cause he never shaved on weekends and wore T-shirts with stains and holes, and a pair of old sneakers.

My dad and Uncle George would take me to watch them play either softball or stickball with the other guys on the block. But, I most remember the ballgames we went to see together. My dad and I would always look forward to those games with George. We would sit and talk sports all day long—and when we spoke on the phone, it was always baseball.

The last game we attended was on Old Timers' Day. I took a picture of Dad and Uncle George. It was the last picture taken of my uncle—he fell sick that following week. My Dad and I went to see him and spent some time at the hospital on the night before his operation. It was the last time we spoke. Sometimes, when I watch baseball, I think of him and the good times we spent at the ballpark. He was baseball. I'm going to miss him very much; we are all going to miss him. We love you. Goodbye, and rest in peace.

Love,

Steven

Connie's words:

This last year, and especially these past few days, we have all been privileged to give acknowledgement and testimony *about our dear George—this kind, gentle, patient soul, "a man among men," who enriched and nurtured so many of us.*

*The stories, the memories we have written down for Terri, Chrissi and Mike, and Claudy and Paul tell of his humor, his professional talents, his love of family and of all God's creatures.*

*George was always ahead of his time; he practiced recycling before it was environmentally correct. You just had to look in his garage or workshop at school; he saved everything for you and for me. He lived for animal rights before it was politically correct. Terri says he could never pass a stray without finding it a home—or, more frequently, keeping it himself.*

*He was a good guy, a guardian angel to so many of us.*

*So I know in my heart that George would want me to thank his guardian angel, his honey, his Theresa, for watching over his welfare and—more importantly—his spirit, this year. George would want you to realize the deep commitment of her love for him. Her strength, her courage! What an inspiration Terri has been to me—to us all this year. She got up every day, she went to work, she cried and she loved—so George could receive all our admiration today. We applaud you, Terri.*

*We pray for George's journey of light and eternal peace and we wish you, Terri, and your loving family a "life of butterflies" and healing.*

And Christopher, so young—just eighteen years old—so dear; as I listen to his words on the tape, so filled with emotion, I am once again moved to gratitude and tears.

Christopher's words:

*We gather today to remember and say goodbye to George Cerrigone. I thought I could share a few memories with you that I have of George . . .*

*Growing up next door to the Cerrigones was an experience in itself. We were always great friends and always looked out for each other. With George, however, this neighborly concern wasn't just friendly—it was fatherly as well. For many years, George was my only every-day father figure, and he filled that role admirably. Whether I wanted to talk to him about school, cars, or our favorite subject—the New York Yankees—he was always available.*

*In addition to George being a great friend, he watched out for our family during some very trying years. Whether it was feeding our cats or fixing our house, George was always there. He never, ever took a day off.*

*In closing, if there was one thing I always wanted to share with George besides saying goodbye—many of us did not have the greatest opportunity to do that—I always thought we would be able to share a Yankees World Series victory. I don't remember the last one—it was in 1978—I was only six. We spent hours complaining about George Steinbrenner and about why Don Mattingly couldn't hit any more. I always assumed that there would be a day, some day in October—hopefully in the near future—that I would be able to come in and say to George, "We finally did it!"*

*I will never forget the games we went to together . . . One opening day, it was brutally cold; it was about forty degrees and raining, and George had to drive—and it wasn't the greatest thing in the world to drive up to the Bronx. We parked and we walked all the way up to our seats—they were in the second-to-the-last row. He didn't complain, and I was pretty young and just wanted to be at the game. Just that he took the day off to go to the game—he never took off from work—made this one of my fondest memories of George. I just wish that we all got the chance to say goodbye.*

A tiny blank booklet, showing a charming picture of a puppy, was also given to each mourner. We asked that every friend and relative record a memory or story of George for us to keep as a remembrance. I have read and reread these keepsakes and they served as a tool for recovery, and a peek back into George's life.

A few of the messages we hold dear are included in this memoir. We laugh riotously when we reread Alison's story of our whitewater rafting trip, on which there was hardly any white water.

Alison writes:
*It was the rafting trip from hell, with me, Claudine, Terri, and George (who, by the way, did most of the rowing while Terri did most of the swearing that "we're never going to get off these damn rocks again"). Thanks to George's humor and ingenuity, we got home safe and sound.*

Eric wrote:
*George, you spoke often of your "Hall of Famers," but did you ever realize what a Hall of Famer you'll always be to me?*

From Susan:
*I remember when I was a little girl at Grandma's house listening to Trini Lopez and Harry Belafonte records with Uncle George.*

From Carolyn:
*I remember George showing up at our new Board of Education work location, and putting just about everyone's bulletin boards up for them.*

From Cousin Elaine:

*I remember how handsome George was in his Army uniform when I was a little kid, but more importantly, I remember his gentle, caring, funny ways, and how he loved his wife and family above everything, with baseball coming in a close second.*

From Rose:

*When we were little kids together (I in my early teens and George about ten), my mother wouldn't let me go to see Frank Sinatra at the Paramount, but she let me go with Georgie as my chaperone. We were fanatical Yankee fans together too.*

From Lorraine:

*When we were fighting to keep our school open, I'll never forget how George went home to get this great big ladder so we could hang our banner, "Don't Close Our School." I think of him and smile.*

From Judy and Joe:

*George was a diamond in the rough—and speaking of diamonds, I can never hear a Neil Diamond song without thinking of George. We love him.*

From Marilyn:

*George, you helped my girls and me through difficult times— whether fixing the boiler, or a shelf, or a lock—always making us feel safe. I'll never forget your telling me to watch you work, because someday I might need to show Terri how to fix things. We'll always be there for your family, as you were to ours.*

From my sister, Josephine:

*I remember how hard George worked at his marriage, achieving more than most partners—he worked and accomplished much and in the end, he evolved and soared like an eagle.*

From Josephine and John:
*We remember George saying, "Nothing can happen to me; I have to watch Daniela grow." We believe he is watching her grow.*

From our daughter Chrissi,
*So many memories . . . The Yankees, working in the basement— doing crafts while Daddy listened to mystery theater—the old movie camera with the bright light on Christmas morning; then there was watching the fireworks from the top of Automotive HS and seeing the NYC marathon from Grandma's block. Of course, I'll never forget watching* My Cousin Vinny *in the movies when Daddy never laughed so hard, and seeing* Father of the Bride *with him shortly before Mike and I got married—he choked up when the bride walked down the aisle with her Dad. Then there was learning to catch, throw, swing (and especially "follow through"), Neil Diamond, and so many more memories I will never ever forget and will always treasure.*

From Claudy:
*Last, but not least, my memory is the best—playing "21" in the driveway.*

During the year of the "silver thread," George evoked dreams among those around him; some shared their special experiences with our family:

From Gail:
*There were several times I dreamed of Uncle George; once he was walking with the dogs in his life that had passed. On*

*the day before his transition, I shared some special time alone with him. On that day I saw his "aura" lift up out of his physical "ill" body and hover over my aunt who was standing beside the bed.*

From Jenn:
*My dream was a conversation between George and me after he passed. I can't remember the exact words, but what was of importance was that he was in such good spirits; I never remember him being so at ease and fulfilled*

From Steve:
*I dreamed of George and asked him what he was doing "up there." He said there were "lots of things for him to fix."*

The gifts of love kept coming; the hundreds of heartfelt cards and words of comfort did sustain me . . .

And from my lifelong friend Barbara and her family:

A gift of trees growing on Long Island in George's honor "for the preservation of the arts."

The funeral was unique, and the funeral director said, "I've never seen so many mourners attend a service on a weekday morning." The icing on our cake is George's headstone. It had to be perfect. It depicts two hearts intertwined—one for him and one for me—with a little cat and puppy on the top of the hearts. In one of the hearts it says, "George Cerrigone, 1934–1993, Husband, Father, Friend, Yankee Fan." At the bottom of the slab, it reads, "Turn on your heart light." How it would tickle him!

So you see, the commemoration of George's life was a series of small acts of disobedience for me; he deserved no less.

From George's "Book of Poems" . . .

## At Christmas

At this time of holiday cheer,
I count my blessings of this ending year,
And of all my memories I cherish on this day,
Is the knowing that our love is here to stay.

So, my sweet, I toast to you,
A Merry Christmas and Happy New Year, too.

~Your loving hubby

# 38

## The Good Times Rolled
## . . . Through the Years

ASCENDING THE DIZZYING steps at the cavernous Madison Square Garden, surrounded by breathless fans, my heart beat faster. It was not because I was climbing stairs, or because we were about to experience a fabulous concert by the iconic Neil Diamond. We were going to see Neil, but also, our daughters had cleverly planned to surprise George for his birthday by showing up at the concert, in nearby seats. A treasured surprise, yes; we just didn't know how treasured it would be. It was only several weeks before George got sick.

Miraculously, again, in August before the September tragedy, we bathed in the warmth of another fun evening together: off to the theater at Jones Beach to see James Taylor, loved by young and old. Our daughters and their friends

Our daughters—all grown up

trooped out to the beachfront theater with George and me. It threatened to storm that evening, and the concert was outdoors. George fashioned raincoats for us out of big black garbage bags. Everyone agreed he was so clever. I'm sure those young people will never forget the night of the black garbage bags and George. I miss his ingenuity in my life. *Where are you, George?*

In a previous "good time" summer, and one of George's last, we had packed up our ancient silver-whiskered dog, Tiffany, with her atrocious breath, and headed up north. With our daughters and their boyfriends, we headed off to

190

Chrissi and Mike—college days

Cooperstown, NY to the Baseball Hall of Fame. How touch-
ingly emotional it was; we not only saw the Hall of Fame,
which was hallowed ground for George, we played basketball,
sliced oars through cold water around the lake, went horseback riding, and ate hotdogs at a real county fair. We laughed
and teased each other; it was prized family time. Gathering in
the aging cottage near the lake, we played board games and
told jokes. On the second day, as we strolled toward the water,
the girls and I saw George emerging from the shallow end of
the lake near the rowboat soaking wet and fully clothed. Paul
and Mike both yelled to us, "We threw George in!" I was horrified, and thought to myself, "That isn't going to endear them
to George." Running toward me and the girls, gasping and
laughing their heads off, they confessed that it was all a joke

and that George had tripped and fallen in the water. We love to remember that funny story whenever we think of him.

Several years earlier, there had been another lucky summer when we drove the precarious mountain roads of the Adirondacks, bound for our friends Connie and Steve's farm with Chrissi, Claudy, and our precious dog, Tiffany. The girls were young teens, and our friends gave us the use of their picturesque sprawling home, secluded on hundreds of acres of forest woodlands. This journey gave us some amazing memories to hold dear. It was idyllic, as we bonded at this most difficult precarious time, when young girls are emerging as young women. Barbequing luscious burgers at the great outdoor grill, we sat around the warm fire, stroking our dog, with Dad telling funny stories until dusk forced us to scatter in every direction as we bolted from the gargantuan bugs that are part of the landscape of Indian Lake.

In a day or two, the Trailways bus had pulled away in a blast of smoke, and our girls were on their way back to Queens, leaving us to bask in time alone for a few more days. I have been able over the years to conjure up this time we shared, because it was magical. Closing my eyes, I can still drink in the scent of the cool, fresh air brushing my face, and smell the sweet wood burning in the outdoor fireplace as we cuddled under the blanket.

In August of 1992, just before George got sick, lucky days thrilled us again as Connie and Steve—along with Connie's kids, Chris and Melissa, and our clan of daughters and boyfriends—came together again for a vacation at Indian Lake. We sped along and bounced over choppy waves in the zooming boat on the scenic lake. Exhilarated, we stopped at tiny deserted islands to picnic. We played board games in the

Paul and Claudine

warm evenings when a thousand stars glinted over the spectacular countryside. Steve had a collection of shotguns, and we took turns shooting at targets—no aiming at any living creature. My girls rode thrilling all-terrain vehicles and we walked deep into the woods with the dogs (by this time, a Reddy Boy puppy was our family dog, as Tiffany had recently gone on to the pet resting place in the clouds) to visit the spiritually peaceful authentic teepee that Connie and Steve had erected. The crescendo of our vacation was an exhilarating show of fantastically colorful fireworks. This glorious family time proved infinitely cherished as the final time we would be together on a family vacation.

The fireworks of 1992 reminded me of a memorable fireworks show George and I had shared with Connie and Steve years earlier. Hundreds of families were expected to dot the spectacular rolling lawns of PepsiCo Corporation in

Westchester County, New York. The outing had been widely advertised as the greatest fireworks show in the county. Connie and Steve had the contract with Pepsi Cola to give a colorful display with all the latest pyrotechnics. Never mind the fact that he was a therapist and she was a teacher; they dabbled in fireworks and this was their big day. It promised to be fine weather, and George and I were going to join our friends late in the day to enjoy the festivities.

Surprisingly, just before 10:00 a.m. on the appointed day, the phone rang insistently in our tiny kitchen. Connie on the other end pleaded for George and me to come up to Purchase right away to help; there had been some glitches in the plans.

When we arrived, Steve was with the organizers of the event making frantic phone calls and having high-level meetings. It seems that the boxed fireworks had not arrived from Indian Lake, where Steve had ordered them from his supplier. Steve's preoccupation with the crisis at hand left Connie to take on the job of digging trenches where the unlit fireworks were to be laid in organized preparation for the big moment. Our mouths fell open as we watched Connie furiously digging, and George's assignment for the day immediately became clear: dig, dig, and dig. I was relegated to babysitter, as Connie's young children were along for the fun.

As we did our jobs, we received sketchy details: The fireworks had to be shipped down quickly, but how? Trucks would take too long. A small plane was secured, and was on its way. All the while, George and Connie dug, dug, and dug. Several hours later, when the fireworks were at the small local airport, trucks were ready to bring the fireworks on the final leg of their trek to the beautifully manicured PepsiCo site. But

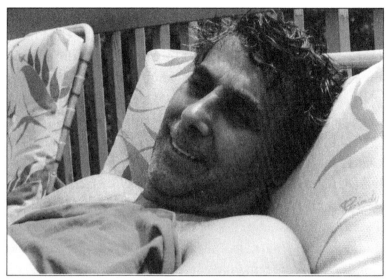

One of the good times

by now, some of the small roads had been blocked, making way for the crowds that were beginning to assemble. Families were arriving for the show, and blankets were being spread out for lavish picnics—many including wine in crystal wine glasses. After all, this was Westchester County, an affluent enclave. I wished I was sitting in a comfortable chair awaiting the beauty of the night, but I was on duty, and George was digging, digging, and digging.

Finally, as twilight began to take over the sky, Connie, Steve, and George were able to pack the various colorful products into the prepared trenches. We had all been working for eight hours. We still had some time, as the show was scheduled for 9:00 p.m.

I had no idea how this slipshod, poorly planned show would turn out. Did they know what they were doing, or would everything blow up prematurely, or perhaps not at all? Was it all timed with precision? Did they have the exact mix of colors and sounds? Who knew? By now, George was filthy, and had actually worn his sneakers through. They had holes in them, and he limped around in pain. George dropped to the ground; his job was finished, and he just gazed up at the night sky. For the second time that day our mouths dropped open, as we heard Steve say, "Does anyone have a match?"

Luckily, someone did have matches, and each and every trench was lit with accuracy. The timing was perfect, the bombs blared, the flares and rockets lit up the sky with elegance and beauty, and spine-tingling music boomed into the night. Twenty minutes later, it was over and we packed up to go home. Success reigned that night on the PepsiCo grounds, and Connie and Steve bought George a new pair of sneakers.

The good times had definitely rolled!

# 39

## Baseball . . . Through the Years

T HE GREY METAL CABINET is tall and imposing, and scarred with age. Sometimes, though, I don't even notice it as I go to the basement to do the wash. When I do open the double doors, hundreds and hundreds of pieces of George look back at me. Sometimes I pick up one dusty book—this time it is a yellowed 1956 official New York Yankees scorebook. It originally cost fifteen cents. Opening the fragile pages, I see the scorebook records a game against the Boston Red Sox, a fearsome foe even today.

George's handwriting appears all over the middle page, which is the actual scoring section of that game. He tried to teach me all the symbols to put in the little boxes, which would tell future generations who batted and whether or not they got a hit or were called out; what player hit to the shortstop, who threw the ball to the second baseman; who got a hit, or perhaps hit a homer. I never quite understood the scoring, but anyone who does—such as his daughters—can see exactly how the game played out. In this particular book, George wrote in the margin that "Nick the Chinaman" went to the game with him. Actually, Nick was not Chinese—he was Italian, and a rather shady figure from the old neighborhood: a bookie.

The book itself reads like a piece of history; Ted Williams and Jim Piersall are listed as playing that day for Boston. They are Hall of Famers, whose feats are recorded in the annals. For New York, Billy Martin, Yogi Berra, and Mickey Mantle are listed, to name a few. Even for me, not a serious baseball fan, the book is thrilling to look through.

On another scorebook, one that I keep safely in my top dresser drawer, I see my own handwriting. Also dated 1956, there is a little heart in which I had written the words "George and Terri." This game is between the Yankees and Kansas City. George wrote in the margin, "'O' play – Stop 9:25," and I see that the game did not go beyond 6 ½ innings—or at least we did not stay. The reason for this is a mystery lost with George.

I continue my trip through the journey of the scorecards. The Yankee scorecard I pick up next to examine is in good condition. It is from a game that had taken place on Sunday, May 13, 1986, and the actual tickets from that game were affixed to its front cover with staples. Yogi Berra stared out at me and the tickets showed George had purchased main level box seats for nine dollars each. The Souvenir Program had cost one dollar. But all that was not unique or special about this particular scorecard. It was the middle section—once again where the actual scoring was recorded—that I turned to, to see if George had notated who attended the game with him that day. Sure enough, this is what I laughingly and joyfully discovered: the handwriting was that of our daughter Claudine, who was sixteen at the time.

Claudine had written the following: "Dad/Claudine," and indicated it was "CAP DAY." It appears that she had written all the players' names in the spaces provided, and that the game had been scored in her handwriting. Noted in the margin was, "Don Mattingly had a virus." She had also written, "I [heart] Ray Smalley, Rick Cerone, Ron Guidry, Don Mattingly." This scorecard is cherished. What a memorable day for me to picture!

Then there's the program from April 23, 1983, with Billy Martin on the cover. That game—according to the notation in Chrissi's handwriting in the middle scoring section—had been attended by the whole family: Mom, Dad, Chrissi, Claudy. Looks like the Yanks lost, if I read the scoring properly.

The scorecard for September 25, 1983—"Impact on Hunger Day"—showed the game that day had been attended by Chris, [cousin?] Carol, and Claudy. Looks like the Yanks won that one.

The last of George's saved scorecards I will mention—although there are dozens more—was one with Don Mattingly, the 1983 American League MVP, on the cover. The card is dated July 18, 1983. Mike Pagliarulo, "Pags," had three hits that day and Mattingly had hit a homerun. The notations are in Chrissi's handwriting, and she had gone to the game with her Daddy. It looks to me like the Yanks won again.

These are the scorecards I cannot seem to part with—they are so precious to my recollections of George's love of baseball.

All of the scorebooks are compelling, and the ads jump out at me: Camel cigarettes, Knickerbocker beer, Old Spice stick deodorant, Beech Nut Gum, Schenley & Seagrams, White Rock, Florsheim Shoes, Chesterfield cigarettes, and dozens of others we recognize from years gone by. Definitely history! I've given many of these keepsakes to my daughters and their families, and to friends who are baseball fans.

Then there are George's sports magazines; of these there are hundreds with pictures of wonderful sports figures gracing their covers, including Joe DiMaggio, Muhammed Ali, Phil Rizzuto, and the "Say Hey Kid," Willie Mays.

Mulling for years over what to do with this collection, I've now discovered a significant opportunity. It was always there, but I guess I was not ready to discover it. I had always asked this friend or that, "What do you think I should do with the collection?" Following a lead, I finally took the simple step to the Internet and I found "Sports Memorabilia Shows," where collectors buy and sell. There are current dates at nearby towns, and I shall go once and for all to get some idea of what I should do with the collection. I feel a weight lifted from my mind and spirit. I know if I do nothing, the books may be lost with the next generation. I must act soon.

George prized baseball as a ballet devotee admires dance. He valued the moves, the intricacies, and subtleties that others missed. George loved baseball when baseball and life itself was more innocent than it is today. Traveling up to Yankee Stadium on the Lexington Avenue line with his brothers or sister—or by himself—when he was a kid was always a thrill. He followed the games throughout the summer, and into the glorious and exciting days of fall. He looked forward to pre-season training as a rite of spring.

Since George died, many times I've heard my son-in-law Paul and my nephews Michael, Peter, and Joseph talk "the baseball talk." "Who's playing for the Yankees this season?" "What are the Mets up to?" They wonder what team "is three games out" and which player might break the record. It tugs at my heartstrings and I get a lump in my throat, because George loved baseball. When Paul and Claudine lived downstairs in the little apartment we fashioned for them after George died, I loved hearing Paul yell at the players as George used to do. I long to hear "the baseball talk" in our house again! I miss it and the missing gives me an empty feeling in the pit of my stomach. Now, it thrills me when my precocious granddaughter Danielle and her dad take in a Yankee game or watch it on television, or when she calls me to tell me the score for a particularly exciting game or one that is disappointing. Or the fun I have when I trek up to Westchester to cheer at the Little League games of Alexandra and Danielle (the pitcher). I always remind them how her grandpa George would have loved watching the games with them.

# 40

## The Animals . . . Over the Years

For Mommy's Birthday

Happy Birthday, Mom, on this your day,
My very best I'd like to say,
You took me in when no one would.
I'd like the world to know you good.
There's just one thing you can do for me:
Keep Chrissi locked up—and safe I'll be.
                              Love,
                              Sam [the dog]

A MEMOIR OF GEORGE and me could not be written without a chapter or two about the animals—so crucial to our lives together. You may be picturing the stereotypical crazy cat lady, keeping dozens of cats in less-than-sanitary conditions, or the old man keeping his ancient nondescript dogs in the junkyard; well, that's not quite George and me. Here is *our* story.

There, on a darkened winter night, we noticed a petite cat with sad eyes huddled in one of the doorways of the tiny church; our hearts sank, for she was barely out of kittenhood. Somehow this delicate cat had found us at the church where George and I were involved in a gritty session of marriage counseling, so we rescued her. "Tabatha," as she became known, was pregnant and frightened. Our friend Evelyn adopted her and so began her devotion to rescued cats.

It had all begun in 1965, after George and I had resumed dating. He arrived at my apartment on a warm spring evening and promptly kicked over my little dog's bowl—water flying everywhere. After that evening, it became apparent that George would treasure my little dog, Oliver, as well as the parade of other dogs and cats soon to enter our lives. To my endless delight, his love for the little creatures blossomed. After we got married, little Oliver died tragically after being hit by an automobile when I failed to tightly shut the front door of our apartment building. He had dashed out to greet George, and was killed. I never felt such sadness and despair before in my life—my first, but not my last, encounter with grief.

The rustic cottage we rented one summer was not elegant, but the tiny lake was cool and the surroundings afforded us a rainbow of wildlife. The birds, plus all manner of bugs, tiny snakes, chipmunks, and frogs, kept us all company—George and I, our two-month-old Christine, and our family dog. This was the setting for our momentous first dog rescue. The sleek young Lab was as black as the midnight sky; we found her wandering near the cottage, appearing to have been abandoned, as so many thousands of animals are each year, in September when families return to the City after summer vacation. We had no experience in the rescue business, as we had purchased our small fox terrier at Macy's pet department, but we could not let this Lab be abandoned again. She was young and friendly, and we decided to bring her back to the city with us, where she was eventually adopted by the sister of a friend.

Before her adoption, however, our quest to decide what to do with "Velvet" had led us down some new paths. We would not deposit her at the ASPCA, as their reputation was poor, but our searching revealed a unique animal adoption group, the New York Animal Adoption Society. The society offered no official shelter; they fostered dogs with various people who agreed to help, or boarded dogs at a veterinarian's office in Manhattan at great expense. The society had been founded and was run by women; they were educated and affluent, and they loved animals and were determined to help strays. So began my pledge to help stray animals; I volunteered with the organization. I was inspired by these women; we forged friendships, and shared experiences that gave me richness that would color my world for years to come. For us, our experience with "Velvet" was when the world of animal rescue and adoption had been truly born.

Our telephone book soon overflowed with names of rescue societies, some of which were supported by wealthy New Yorkers. We became friends with like-minded doctors, lawyers, artists, and actors, and worked side by side with them to assist in sometimes-exhilarating rescue missions.

All the while, George religiously walked our own two dogs a mile or so through the deserted late night streets near the

East River, where he fed half a dozen stray dogs, each and every day. Some success stories unfolded as we placed several dogs in good and loving homes. When we moved to our house in Flushing, George continued feeding strays, except now it was the little kitties being fed. In my mind's eye, George is walking to the end of our driveway, reminding me of the Pied Piper as almost a dozen stray cats of all colors gather near our garage at the back of the house waiting for their breakfast. Trudging out back in rain or shine—and especially in snow-storms—he fed these cats for years.

When George got sick, he said, "Please take care of my cats," and I reassured him that I would. At that time, there were seven cats we called our own—no longer strays—plus the usual ten or more strays awaiting food at the end of our driveway. When George died, I continued to fulfill my promise, although at times, the chore seemed almost insurmountable, and I always felt George's absence acutely as I took his place. Ten years after George died only one stray remained at the garage door. "Chubby" soon found his way into the house, where he remained until he passed away. Others of our house cats have also followed George to the great backyard in the sky; now, I am down to four.

The mourning for George as our animal undertaker is all the more poignant when I remember sorrowful phone calls from friends and family, "George, can you help us?" George would descend the stairs to his basement to craft a tiny coffin for each pet. They could be buried in their own yard or in ours, where we had a little burial ground out back. Now, the precious pets no longer have someone to lovingly craft them a final resting place.

Terri with the exceptional Reddy Boy

## My Special Boy "Red" . . . 1990-2005

I N THE SUMMER OF 1990, as my niece Diane was gazing out of her seventh floor window, she saw a skinny dog just as a car hit him, and she watched as he hobbled on his broken leg. The ASPCA came to collect the injured dog and Diane sadly watched the truck disappear; what would happen to him? She and her mom—my sister, Josephine—couldn't bear what the answer to that question might be, so Diane's husband took off to the Brooklyn shelter where the dog had been taken. Steve demanded that they give the dog to him. "We have to keep the dog for twenty-four hours; come back tomorrow," was the reply. The dog would suffer there with his broken leg for twenty-four hours, so Steve grabbed the guy at the desk by the collar: "Bring the f—-ing dog out NOW," Steve commanded.

They thought they might be dealing with a "crazy man" so out came the injured dog. The dog promptly peed on the floor—and with that, they left the building.

"Could we foster the rescued dog when he is released from the vet until he finds a home?" I asked George. "Sure," George said, and so the young, silky haired, white-and-rust Brittany spaniel came bounding in with the great white cast on his leg, destined to live at our house until the end of his days. We named him "Red." He was my constant companion in the years after George died, until recently, at age fifteen, when he became very ill and joined George in whatever hereafter exists.

## Red

I've begun to write for Red the boy,
Who, from the beginning, brought so much joy.

He's not so obedient, or even terribly smart,
But his loyalty and sweetness—he's made those an art.

I watch him with the children, his colorful white
    and red,
And oh, we're all so attached to that Brittany . . . "Fred."

I'm so glad we've known him, from "Tiffany" to "Dudley
    the Great,"
And all the little ones who just love to imitate.

He's amazed me by tricking us to get off the couch,
So he can get into *his* spot and just rest and slouch.

He drifts, he dreams of days long ago,
When he bounded the yard in a great flow—
Even with the cast on his broken leg,
He flew, he raced, he never ran slow.

Now he hobbles after his pals Blackie & Willie,
Trying to remember all the fuss and willy-nilly,

We take for granted the puppy days—everyone's young
    and fast,
Suddenly life's in slow motion—we're old, he's old . .
And each move seems as though it might be the last.

It's precious though, we need to see; hang on to the
    sweet things,
The precious days, his and ours, then we'll take what
    life brings!

He's part of our lives, how will we ever let him go free?
We'll treasure each memory and picture his furry glee.

The softest fur we've ever known,
The greatest honor he is to own.

Except he owns us, and we *share* each other's lives,
Reddy Boy, one of many special pets, what a gift, what
    a prize!

~By Terri (Red's best pal) 2004

There are many other unique and memorable animal rescue stories in George's repertoire that might fill another volume. His good work with animals did not stop with feeding strays and caring for our own pets. He picked up abandoned and abused animals, and helped capture lost ones or those simply needing help. He stopped at nothing to rescue animals, at times waiting hours for one to appear that we had been attempting to trap, and even being bitten by a frightened dog or cat once or twice.

We saved a stunning German shepherd from a grimy bar; he found a home with a lovely couple in Manhattan. There were little dogs and all manner of medium-sized dogs. One particularly regal dog found a forever home with a retired school principal in Bronxville; we told her he was a Basenji mix–quite an exotic breed—and perhaps he was. A chubby basset hound found his place with an Orthodox family in Brighton Beach. We often fostered a pup in our home for weeks until it found a forever home, and some just came to stay. George never said "No" to me about an animal—never, ever! Our own menagerie included cats: Sox, Tigger, Esmerelda, Rocky, Jake, Ginger, Peaches, 'Fraidy Cat, Morris, Dusty, and Mandy, among others who came and went; and, of course, our soulful dogs: Sam, June, Tiffany, and finally, Red. "Are you crazy?" we were asked on numerous occasions. "All those cats?" people asked. Who cared, we were a team.

George was inspired and moved to write poems about animals, and although the old life we shared exists as if a dream, I can hold onto that dream in his sweet poems. The poetry was the voice of his soul. There you have it—the stereotypes of the crazy animal rescuers, and a poem by George to celebrate the animals:

December 11, 1975
To: Christine and Claudine

## Just a Dog Named Sam

She's only a mutt, no different than most,
Who eats almost every chance she can
And has one ear that is always bent,
Just a dog named Sam.

She can't do tricks that would bring her fame,
'Cept maybe put her paw in your hand;
That's not much to say for her side,
Just a dog named Sam.

She's always in the way, lying around,
Not much for looks, 'cept for her color—golden tan.
And barks a lot, at almost every thing,
Just a dog named Sam.

And now we hear she hasn't got far to go,
And soon will go into the land,
Then she won't be around any more,
Just a dog named Sam

Some may say, "So what," she's gone,
It's not like the death of a man.
It's only a dog that you can replace,
Just a dog named Sam.

And maybe they're right—she'll be gone, *good-bye,*
'Cept . . . when she's not at hand
There'll be an emptiness at our house,
For just a dog named Sam.

~Your Father

# 41

## Kathryn . . . 1953, 1958

AS WE ASCENDED THE grimy underground steps at 42nd Street in Manhattan, I gazed at Kathryn's beautiful legs, the seams of her black sheer stockings tracing the lovely shape of her slim ankles. I was in awe. At perhaps fourteen, I was on my way to what would be the first of many spectacular Broadway musicals I would come to adore.

Kathryn was my older brother Bobby's friend, eight years older than me and worldly. She was everything I wanted to be. An Italian-American beauty with long raven hair, she was bright and Bohemian. Although she was my older brother's friend, she had taken me under her wing one day when I tagged along as he visited her at her parents' apartment. I was so enthusiastic and enthralled with her—wanting to know all about her interesting life—that she couldn't have helped but respond by becoming my mentor.

Kathryn worked for a Broadway talent agency, and knew fascinating people—including an older cigar-smoking guy she introduced me to that night; she said he was a friend. She was building a career in this field making connections, and I suppose he was one of those. This night, we were on our way to see *The Boyfriend,* starring—in her Broadway debut—the young and talented Julie Andrews. It was a perfect show for me, a young burgeoning dancer, developing teen, and child excited by life. My eyes widened and my heart beat faster as the curtain was raised on the brightly lit stage. I had never seen such a spectacle, and musical comedy would forever after hold a special place in my heart. And although I had never heard of Julie Andrews before that night, I would recall with pride later in life that I had seen her perform so young, when she first burst upon the New York stage.

I only recollect these snippets of memory about Kathryn: we loved the play, we met her attractive friends, and I wanted to dress like she did—complete with black stockings, the Bohemian skirt, and big gold earrings. I don't remember seeing Kathryn too many times after that—I was busy growing up and finding "better things" to do with my own teenage friends. I would hear about her from my brother from time to time, and always I imagined I'd see her soon, and that we would share girl secrets as we did on that night we had shared *The Boyfriend* together.

That was not to be. One day a few years later, my brother was given devastating news: Kathryn and her young, handsome boyfriend had been killed tragically—while traveling on the Long Island Expressway, another driver had sailed over the divider and crushed their indefensible little Volkswagen "Bug."

I was overwhelmed by the heartbreaking news. I did not and could not attend the funeral for Kathryn. I'm not sure why I made this choice, except that I was young. My youth kept me away from the service and from the shock of seeing my beautiful friend in the casket. Although I have since questioned my decision, perhaps I was right to keep Kathryn only in my memory of the storied night, entranced by the lights of Broadway, thrilled to the showing of *The Boyfriend* on the Manhattan stage. I forever keep her—young and alive and sparkling in her Bohemian clothes—delighting in the short time we had together, and envisioning her in that freeze frame of a happy time in both our lives.

# 42

# Years Ago When I Was Happy ... 1969

GIANT SIZED, LUMINESCENT flakes fell noiselessly. It seemed there was nothing as silent as this snowy night. It was dark, but the sparkling white flakes lit up the sky as I walked the few short blocks from my little apartment in Astoria, Queens, to my older sister Jo's apartment where she lived with her husband, Mike, and her young daughters, Diane and Carol.

Diane and Carol, two of my precious nieces, were the joys of my life, as they had been born when I was an impressionable teenager, my heart bursting with enthusiasm for life. Babies had held a fascination for me since my first niece, Paula, was born when I was just thirteen. I could not believe how much I could love someone—it was pure devotion. I was "Auntie," and we looked forward to seeing each other regularly; I often slept overnight for extra fun. After Paula, came Diane, then Valerie, and then Carol was born, and—last, but not least—Gail. These little girls were adored not only for their charms, but because they were my sister Jo's and my older brother Bob's children. Jo and Bob were my best friends and mentors.

Jo had strawberry blonde hair, and was slender and beautiful. She was glamorous and had always had boyfriends at her heels. She had an adventurous side—as a young teen, she followed the boys for a swim in the East River to prove she was as brave as they were. Jo forever danced to her own music. She was tender to her children and mine, and to all the four-legged friends who came across her path.

When she married the handsome Michael, I was sad that she left me behind. I wanted to go with her. She was so good to me; she took me with her to the beach and to the "Greeks," the soda shop where she socialized with friends—lovely things for an older sister to do.

My older brother, Bob—ten years older than me—had always been my protector. I cried when he was off to the Army when I was only eight. Later I blossomed under his mentoring when I was a teenager. He was active in the Oil Chemical and Atomic Workers International Union, organizing for the company he worked for, and I excitedly rode along in the bus with all the other union members as they fought for workers' rights and attended rallies, while raising my awareness and building the foundation for my current political beliefs.

On that snowy evening so long ago, contentment and peace filled me. The baby was home with George and the dogs—all of them cozily curled up together, spectators to the winter snowstorm. The streets were covered with a silvery

Jo, Bob, and Theresa—having fun together

sheen, and cars could slide about on the slick roads, so few passed. How glorious to walk the short distance in my furry boots, muffler, and mittens, as I envisioned the warmth of my sister's home and the joyfulness of the young, vivacious girls who would soon greet me.

Memories of that silent evening remind me that Josephine died fourteen years ago at a youthful sixty-five and George died twenty years ago at only fifty-eight. Now two bright lights have gone out of my life. Two of my best friends, Josephine and George, are as silent as the snowy night and I only hope they are as peaceful. I long to hear their voices at the other end of the telephone and to see their faces; but their voices have been stilled.

Now I recall the precious moments we all shared before death quieted their earthly voices. I still share the good times with my treasured nieces and my brother when we talk, almost every day. Through these marvelous memories and precious family ties I can bring their voices out of the silence once more.

## Contemplating Death . . . 1992 and Beyond

THE SIMPLE LITTLE white book at my fingertips became a lifeline as I searched for answers to the devastation that had suddenly invaded my world. In the darkest hours and in the midst of all the tears, I was comforted by Native American teachings, and the inspiring words from The Kashi Foundation: "Teach of death simply so you can live." The Kashi Foundation explains that "to dance with death is to befriend death and find in yourself your own particular meaning of life and life's dreams." Further, it teaches, "We who have the honor of being there when a loved one is dying know that this is the greatest intimacy possible. To be able to share that moment is a great honor."

Now, when I am in the mood to fantasize, I picture meeting George in the hereafter, as well as reuniting with my mother, father, my sister, Jo, and our pets. As some have described the glorious happy reunion of the hereafter, it looks warm and familiar when it comes to me in my dreams. I have read, "It is only a moment for those on the other side, until they are reunited with their loved ones" and it helps me deal with George's disappearance from our lives. And if on "the other side" there is only death and nothingness, then that's all right too. I can only live this time in the very best way I can. Either way, I am not afraid, although I'm not ready to go just yet. Too many wonderful moments, hours, days, and years are left to revel in the joy that is life, and most especially in the company of cherished children, grandchildren, pets, and friends.

# 43

## The Spiritual and the Uplifting
. . . Christmas 1992

## A Birthday Celebration . . . 1994

*Now and forever, I will always think of you . . .*
~words and music by Carole King

T HE SANCTUARY DAZZLED with the lights of dozens
of candles and brilliant red poinsettias, overwhelming
the small alter on this, my first Christmas without
George. The candlelight service at the tiny church in Valley
Stream beckoned, as "greeters" took my hand with a warm
smile and a tender touch. Dramatic stained glass windows
reflected the candlelight. Peace wrapped around me as I
listened to the calming words spoken by the pastor, and
piano melodies accompanied the congregation in their
joyful renditions of the sweet songs. It touched me and I
found comfort at this tiny church for years to come, with

its hushed and tranquil meditation garden in back, and fellowship after each service. It was called "Unity."

It was a place to cry and make some sense of our tragedy. Nearby was Connie—my friend who had visited George with me countless times in the year before he died, who had driven me everywhere I needed to be driven, who was by my side during the planning of the funeral and memorial services for George. Connie had not only encouraged me on every step of my unusual journey, she became my lifeline—the best friend anyone could have, then and now. Connie sang loudly at the Unity services, and put her arms around me when I cried during the hymns.

In July 1994, almost a year after George died, this spiritual cocoon was the setting for a memorial for George. It was the occasion of what would have been his sixtieth birthday. On that day, family and friends gathered to remember him. Still grieving and refusing to forget, I wanted a memorial/birthday service to be celebrated. On a hot July day, the simple quiet sanctuary radiated with love and sadness.

After twenty years, once again and at long last, I decided to listen to the voices from the past—the voices of that service so carefully planned. As I played the old tape, I was brought back to the very day, the very place where sunlight streamed through familiar stained glass windows that I had gazed at with eyes brimming that first year after George died.

Reverend Joe Rowe officiated at this special celebratory service. I was struck at how personally he had spoken of George, often mentioning our daughters by name and reminding us of all the wonderful experiences we had all shared: the details of George's love of animals and of baseball, George's helpfulness to all our friends and relatives . . . our camping weekends with the Girl Scouts, our glorious vacation in scenic Colorado (where we had visited Aspen and sung John Denver songs), the concerts we attended together, the family gatherings and picnics in our backyard, George's love of little children—of course, the Fourth of July at Pepsico, and George's poem dedicated to Claudine on the back of the day's program.

Our young friend Jennifer sang in a clear and touching voice the song "Now and Forever," from the movie *A League of Their Own.* Having watched the movie numerous times, I knew how much George would have loved this film about baseball and women. "It's a perfect song, and it tells yours and Daddy's story," my daughter Chrissi had said—to which I replied, "It does feel as though it were written just for us . . . *Now and forever you are a part of me, and the memory cuts like a knife. We had a moment, just one moment.*"

Now in 2013, as I listened to Jenny on the tape, the tears began anew and I felt awed that these words were the culmination of our story. I could not believe how perfectly befitting they were: *Now and forever, I will always think of you.*

At the service, Jenny sang "Heartlight," from the movie *ET: But now that he had to go away, I still feel the words that he might say . . . I'll be right here if you should call me . . . .*

The congregation sang "Sonlight," my favorite hymn, faces aglow with the light of many candles flickering.

My friend Connie shared the piece "Sorrow to Remembrance," taken from the book *Gentle Closings: How to Say Goodbye to Someone You Love,* by Ted Menten.

Connie's words told a story of teaching children—fittingly, as Connie is a teacher—teaching and inspiring children to bring remembrance to their grief, and comforting them with the assurance that through remembrance, their loved one will always be with them. Connie's story was one we all needed to hear on that July night in 1994 in honor of George's birthday.

The memorial represented George's final release from the silver thread.

It helped me grab onto my own thread of happiness and peace.

# 44

## Moving Still Further . . . 1995

A GARAGE FILLED TO THE brim with stuff, and a basement cluttered and chaotic stood as a monument to George's own distinct personality. But when he died, I needed to improve my finances creatively so that I could remain in the home we shared, which I loved. My soon-to-be son-in-law, Paul, suggested we turn George's messy, crazy basement into a home for my daughter and him, eventually to rent as a little apartment. We did just that, and so I had three more years of delicious company as Claudine and Paul and Dudley—Paul's big, friendly, fluffy-white dog—lived downstairs.

We laughed as we cleared out the outrageous basement that had been George's. Hilarity ensued when we found things George had fixed or built, into which dozens of extra nails has been pounded. When George built or fixed something, he wanted it to last. I felt sad as we cleared and cleaned and got rid of all the "stuff" that George had lovingly accumulated. And did he accumulate "stuff!" Not knowing what most of it was, I knew he would forgive me if most of his basement "stuff" needed to go in order for our children to live there. Dumpster after dumpster was filled from the basement and the garage. The day the dumpsters were to be collected, I rushed out of the house, as I couldn't look at it all being taken away. Later that day as Connie and I drove slowly past the house, Paul yelled out, "Keep going—it's not finished yet." The whole purging process felt a little sacrilegious, but the house was to be for the living, and so it is. The basement is a charming, spacious apartment, and there is still so much of George within the house. That's why I don't want to leave.

Then, on September 21, 1996, another momentous September date, our younger daughter, Claudine, George's special girl, got married. When she married Paul, she was the very vision of a fairy princess, with her dark tresses piled up in curls that nestled around her sparkling tiara. Once again, I alone walked my daughter down the aisle, in our familiar neighborhood church. It was a glorious wedding, bringing with it a taste of the bittersweet, without our George. Claudine and Paul lived in that cute, little basement apartment for three years, and sometimes as I heard Paul scream and yell as he often did while watching football or baseball, my heart stopped just a little, because he sounded so much like George had as he watched the games.

Now years later, I gaze at the basement, and even though it has been transformed, I still think of it as George's basement—

Claudine and Paul

his sanctuary, his place to get away from me, his to dream up small inventions or be Mr. Fix-It—his world. Most of George's treasures there had to go, as have other treasures around the house, just worn out: the cabinet with two little drawers and shelves he fashioned for the yard, finally rocking and split, just fell to pieces. Many of his tools remain in the laundry room and garage, silent and unknown by all of us as to their use.

## The Old Shaving Brush . . . 2011

THE OLD SHAVING brush greets me every morning as I open the medicine cabinet. Sometimes I don't even notice it, and other times it jumps out, reminding me that I decided long ago never to let it go. Yes, I decided it was the one possession belonging to George that I would never part with—this, so personal an object. Many objects have been discarded and other precious items have been kept lovingly. But this, a simple unimportant shaving brush—not precious, just an old shaving brush—is here to stay.

Other important objects, such as our numerous old photographs, stare back at me from every room: George—as a young man, at bat, swinging at a perfect pitch; in his Army uniform, strikingly handsome and so young; with our girls, beaming proudly; at a family party, tenderly kissing me. These photos I could never part with, no question—but the shaving brush? A small and insignificant item—but oh, how dear. After all, George twirled it round and round, making circles on his lovely beard. His beard so dark—I loved how it rubbed my face. Sometimes during vacations, he wouldn't shave and it grew soft and luxuriant. And then off it would go—he'd be back to being clean-shaven.

A particularly bittersweet moment was when I decided our original bedroom set had to go, giving way to a light, feminine new décor. I gave the furniture to a young couple, and so I reasoned it had a new life with a loving family.

Other rooms have undergone changes: the den is different now—containing an efficient computer, a new TV, couch, recliner, and rug—from the den as it used to be; only the special print of Joe DiMaggio and his endless books on sports and movie trivia remain.

Still, the shaving brush—so personal—having touched both his hands and face, remains almost alive. The old-fashioned shaving brush, small and cute, could stay with me wherever I go. Amazingly, the bristles do not fall out and it does not rot; it still feels soft, not intruding on my life, not accusing me of never moving on. It's unobtrusive and takes up little room. It reminds me of my father, who had a similar brush—how nice. So the shaving brush creates a linear memory from my father to George. It's not a beautiful sight for visitors to enjoy; it's just for me, special, tender—and again, so personal. Useless, you may say—perhaps, unless I decide to use it to lather my legs for shaving. Why not? I will think of it as a hundred kisses.

# 45

## My Working Life and Its Gifts
. . . 1962

THIS IS A TALE OF GRANDEUR and betrayal. Returning from the episode in my young life when I was
living in Miami Beach and attempting to rekindle
my romance with Ray, I found myself back in New York. I
needed a job. Happy to be home, for I missed my family, still,
I longed for the pink sand and starlit nights. Living in Miami
Beach for a year had been a dream, and this was real life.

Answering the ad for an executive secretary, I stared up at
the tall, grey, imposing Time Life Building. It wasn't a pretty
building, but the salary offered was more than I ever earned.
Being an excellent secretary, I, in my interview suit, arrived
enthusiastically for the meeting.

The slender, conservatively dressed older woman greeted
me—she was around fifty at the time; I was twenty-two.

Formalities concluded. I suppose she liked me, because I got the job.

I learned that this company produced absolutely nothing, except money. All business was transacted on the telephone, or by fax; the company imported chrome ore from South Africa, which they subsequently sold to companies in the US. Never understanding exactly how all this was achieved, I took shorthand, typed letters, and was responsible for the myriad tasks of a one-girl office. It was a little lonely.

Making clean money, Mr. K, president and CEO, was the middleman. He occupied the large, extravagant office, sitting behind a massive mahogany desk. I discovered that the woman who had interviewed me was the wife of this middle-aged overfed executive.

Most of my directions came from Mrs. K; Mr. K was Dutch or German—he had an accent, and rarely emerged from his office cocoon where he was conducting business. As he spoke to me little, except for the dictation of letters, I was intimidated; later, though, he revealed his rather agreeable nature. Eventually, as the months passed, Mrs. K and I shared personal stories and she confided the following: When she was thirty, she had gathered up the money she possessed and taken a glamorous trip to Europe, determined to find a rich husband. Her single-mindedness paid off, as she met Mr. K, and their union was born. Returning to the states together, the business they operated was exceptionally lucrative.

With money rolling in, they decided to invest in another venture: the owning and raising of Black Angus cattle, in the upscale community of Rhinebeck, New York. On weekends, they retreated to a magnificent old farmhouse they had grandly restored.

I was young and warm and spirited, and I suppose they liked having me around; they began to treat me as a daughter. After several months, they invited me to dinner at expensive Manhattan restaurants that boasted radiant chandeliers and gleaming silver, where they strongly suggested I taste escargot. Soon thereafter, I was invited to spend the weekend at the farm.

Arriving on the night of a near-blizzard snowstorm, I can never forget gazing out the huge glass windows onto the dazzling white flakes blanketing the rolling hills of the farm as we sat cozily in the graceful dining room, being waited on by a kind, nervous young housemaid. I noticed that Mrs. K was demanding—as I was to experience myself—and felt, even as a guest in their home, that tension sat alongside grandeur.

The grand tour of their home revealed that it had been restored with the assistance of prestigious decorators, and the results were flawless. It was the picture of grandeur with the elegance of country charm—no detail left to chance. Expensive antiques decorated every room, mahogany floors shone, and glowing fireplaces dotted the rooms; each space had its own thick brilliant Persian rug. I was shown to my beautiful room, with its soft, downy bed and cozy electric blanket—still, I felt apprehension as Mrs. K watched my every move.

But the next morning, I was treated to an unforgettable experience. The couple woke me at dawn to be present when a steaming little calf slipped out into the world. I was ecstatic. I was drawn in by the soulful eyes of those sleekly jet black, extremely valuable cows. I loved the animals.

Happy to return to my parents' tiny apartment in Jackson Heights, furnished in early Sears Roebuck, and where I slept on the pullout couch in the living room, I was at home. Still, I accepted another invitation to the farm; this springtime weekend showed off the green velvet carpet beautifying the hillside. It was during this stay that Mrs. K began to tell me how to behave, admonishing me not to talk to the young man at the filling station. She also suggested that I cut my hair; it was too long. Attending the Rhinebeck State Fair with a young man who worked at the farm, I realized I was more comfortable with him and with the young caretaking family on the farm, with their children and dogs. Mrs. K had nothing to do with them, and actually told me she cared little for children or dogs. Once more, I was happy to return to the City.

It was around the one-year anniversary of my working at this office that the betrayal took place. Mrs. K was out of the office, and I typed a letter to my friend in California, complaining that my boss was overbearing and difficult. When I was out sick the next day, Mrs. K obviously must have rifled through my desk and found the letter, which I had mistakenly left in the drawer. She called me at home and fired me. I suppose she felt betrayed, but I had been betrayed, too— she had read my personal letter. When I applied for unemployment insurance, Mrs. K demanded that it be denied. Appearing at the unemployment office for a hearing, I was asked, "Did Mr. K make advances to you?" I said, "No, he was very pleasant," and I related the story of the letter. My unemployment payments were allowed, and I was once again looking for a job in Manhattan.

# All The Rest of My Working Life and Its Gifts … Through the Years

M Y CAREER WAS amazing. Yes, it was a career. Secretaries are rarely thought of as professionals; we may be called executive assistants, but we all begin as secretaries. I took to shorthand like a duck to water, copying the little squiggly lines when my sister studied it in high school. I practiced diligently and it has become another language for me. I had found my working life. Now, over seventy, I can't stop myself from thinking in shorthand. I secretly write the words I hear—in the air or on my leg or in my head—in those squiggly symbols.

I was fifteen when I lied about my age and got my first clerical job. My intention was to stay for the summer, and by the time they investigated me, the summer was almost over and I sheepishly left. It was mindless paperwork that I actually liked. Perhaps the idea of it—dressing cutely, joining the throngs on the train, taking lunch in the cafeteria, and, of course, getting a paycheck—all intrigued me.

In my high school senior year, I worked at a printing company on Houston Street. I arrived after school and did my homework while on duty at the old-fashioned switchboard with its blinking lights and crisscrossed wires that seemed like so many snakes on a board. Mastering it would rival the high-tech devices of today. I was the only telephone operator who sat in the swivel chair with one leg tucked under me, wearing saddle shoes and bobby sox. I loved working there and I loved my working life. After being graduated from high school, the printing company took me on full time.

235

The next job on my personal ladder of success was with the Oil, Chemical, and Atomic Workers (OCAW) International Union as secretary to the Eastern Head of Operations. I raptly listened to tales of the days in Texas when strikers were beaten as they attempted to unionize. Since high school days, I had accompanied my brother, Bob, to star-studded union rallies supporting strikes against chemical companies. It was at one of the rallies that I met Tony Mazzocchi, president of the local, now the subject of a book entitled *The Man Who Hated Work and Loved Labor – The Life and Times of Tony Mazzocchi.* Tony served as Legislative Director of OCAW in Washington, DC where he headed the fight that led to the passage of the Occupational Safety and Health Act, alongside nuclear whistleblower Karen Silkwood. I found my working life intersected with my social consciousness.

Around that same time, there was a day I turned the corner of the block where the union office was located and ran into Paul Newman, then starring in *Sweet Bird of Youth.* Although not as significant, the encounter was thrilling and memorable, and certainly worth honorable mention in my memoir.

Stints followed as secretary at a prestigious architectural design company where I worked alongside architects and artists as they brought their designs to life, and then as secretary to the husband-and-wife team who imported chrome ore from Rhodesia and South Africa and resold it in America and who also raised the Black Angus cattle in upstate New York that I have spoken of earlier in this chapter. And, too, there had been the colorful journey I had experienced earlier in life as secretary to the head of the kosher hotel in Miami Beach. I found my working life brought me adventures.

My job as executive assistant to the president of the French and Italian knitwear firm was defining for me. We were located in the garment center—the hub of the fashion world. My boss, a handsome Frenchman, had "private meetings" in his office with models who visited our office. It took me a while to understand what was going on behind closed doors.

Memories of my time with this fascinating company are of the magnificent fabrics with their unique designs and colors, the dramatic fashions, and the romance of the French language all filling my senses each day I stepped off the elevator. During my time there, I re-met George, got engaged, got married, and became pregnant.

Before I left that job, I was called upon to be commentator of our annual fashion show at the glamorous Hampshire House Hotel overlooking Central Park. I introduced each of our beautiful designs, worn by famous models of the day, as they strode the runway for potential buyers. I had found my speaking voice. It was fantastic and fun and I stayed with the knitwear firm until the week before I gave birth.

Also worth honorable mention is the fact that I met a lovely young English girl at that firm. Her name was Margaret, and we became friends. She was the sister of Paul Anka's wife, whom we knew as "Anne," and we all went off to the Copacabana one enchanting evening where we met Paul backstage. My child, Christine, was born in the same week as Paul and Anne's first daughter, and Anne and I once chatted on the phone while taking care of our new babies.

George encouraged me to "Take the test for school secretary." Wasn't he clever?! I did become a school secretary, but later I was asked to take a civil service position with the new head of special education in Queens, Richard Crowley. My time with Richard Crowley, Deputy Assistant Superintendent for the Queens Division, was magical; we—his friends and co-workers—called it "Camelot" because of the deep dedication and courage he brought to our borough, and how it reminded us of the historical time of JFK so many years ago. It truly was Camelot, because it ended. Richard left the board, retiring to regain his health, and the following year I lost my George.

My final assignment with the Board of Education was a miracle. I had been demoted because of budget cuts, a common occurrence in Board of Education annals. The demotion came just as George died, and I was fearful. I was away for the weekend with my sister, Jo, when my daughter called me: "A high-level person at the Board of Education wants to meet you to discuss an executive assistant position." I found out that I had been recommended for the job by a colleague in Queens. After the interview with the Vice President of the New York City Board of Education, Dr. Irene Impellizzeri, I was informed that I had been awarded the position.

My career ended after twenty years with the Board of Education. My position—which for the last six years had been with the Central Board, working for Dr. Impellizzeri—carried a good salary and benefit package. More importantly, this famous, delightful, and intelligent woman became my mentor in many areas of life, including writing—a link to my now-fulfilling passion. Leaving that job and the world of work was an extraordinary gift. I would no longer have to drive each morning on the horrendous Brooklyn Queens Expressway. I had now found the new and wonderful world of the retired.

# 46

# I Loved Doris Day

LONG BEFORE I FELL in love with Neil Diamond, John Denver, and Harry Belafonte—all of whom I became acquainted with because of George—I loved Doris Day.

She was sweet, sassy, sexy, and sang and danced in those big lavish musical comedies of long ago. I can't remember when I didn't want to be in musicals. From the first Betty Grable, Fred Astaire, Gene Kelly—and yes, Doris Day—movies on that big Technicolor screen, I wanted to sing, dance, and act. That was my dream.

I recall vividly, as a really young child—perhaps five years old—being taken to a religious play at Fordham University. It was then that I fell in love with live theater. I came home and performed the assorted characters in front of the sofa for my make-believe audience. Later, I refined my tastes to musical comedies; they were irresistible. My love for movies and plays continued throughout my teen years and on into young womanhood.

Once in elementary school, I was chosen to be one of the presenters at a showing of paintings given to our school. I was to introduce the painting, giving a brief history of the artist to visitors as they viewed the various works of art adorning our auditorium. It seems I was not afraid of public speaking, which is of course akin to acting. When I was chosen to present the speech at eighth grade graduation, I didn't hesitate to give a spirited talk.

My love for musicals included a passion for the extravagant costumes parading across the screen—those floating, tulle-laden, pouffed Cinderella dresses. So, when I was fifteen and invited by Lennie, an older neighborhood boy, to attend his prom, I was ecstatic. Off I went in a pink strapless tulle gown borrowed from my sister's friend. I thought, then and there, that my dream had come true, being able to wear that dress.

As a young woman, my performing was elevated to ballet lessons. I took ballet until the week before I gave birth to my first child. Even with the best intentions to return to ballet lessons, performing, for me, was thwarted by life—with marriage, babies, and work, it took a back seat. The yearning stayed secretly in my heart.

I had another opportunity for a bit of performing when I was an announcer for a huge, glitzy fashion show held for buyers at the elegant Hampshire House near Central Park, during my stint with the French and Italian knitwear firm.

Later, when I was employed by the Board of Education, a clowning experience I had at St. John's University for a Special Olympics event was exhilarating, and so another piece of the dream had come true.

My ultimate acting/dancing/princess dream came true when I was in my forties. My children had attended dancing school for several years when the director decided to have a moms' class, which I eagerly joined. We practiced tap and jazz and had fun, but we wanted to perform. She said she would choreograph some numbers for us if we agreed to go on stage at the end of the performance dressed in crazy animal costumes to greet the children and delight the audience in general. No problem. We wanted to perform. We practiced hard and chose our sparkly costumes. For the tap number, it was a sexy black-and-white very short outfit, covered with sequins and spangles and completed with top hats and canes. The other costume was a clingy, slinky number in electric blue for the jazz piece. We were ready to go.

About three weeks before the show, I picked my daughter up at a friend's house. As I entered the building, a young man, strong and big, slammed through the door and landed on my toe, which turned out to be badly bruised and broken. I cried, and couldn't stop crying, because it hurt so much, and also because I might not be able to dance in the show. Luckily, we taped it up, and it healed just enough for me to go on with the performance. We were a huge success, and I reveled in the music, the performing, and the applause, with pictures to prove I actually danced in public wearing those sexy costumes. I instructed George to make sure to cheer and whistle for me. He said, "You know, I am your very biggest fan," and so he was, when I made my dancing debut. I look back on my brief dancing career as my dream come true.

My idol, Doris Day, is more my idol today than ever before. You see, she is the founder and CEO of the Doris Day Animal League, a humanitarian and rescue organization based in Washington, DC. It is also a lobby group for the humane treatment of animals. I think it ironic that we are kindred spirits in our endeavors, as I have been involved in animal rescue for many years. And so my dream has doubly come true, because I have a special connection—a more important connection—to "my" Doris, aside from my love of her musical performances. That's a dream I'm proud to have come true.

# 47

# Loss . . . Through the Years

CLIMBING OUT OF THE dark pit of loss has become a studied art for me. At the beginning, there were only moments, then hours, then days, when cautiously climbing out was possible. Supreme effort pulled me together for special times like my daughter's wedding, only four weeks after George fell ill, where I was disbelieving—how could I be here, celebrating, without the father of the bride? It was a shock as I tearfully listened to the two clergymen speaking the happy words. Holidays and times with the young children in my life cut off my feelings of loss, temporarily. At the beginning, I refused to go to couples' parties, and weddings were especially painful. But as weeks, months, and years slipped by, I ventured out more often, staying in the joy of living each day longer and longer.

But there are times I am dragged back to the deep and poignant feeling of loss. Watching middle-aged couples, heads close together, commenting on the sights during a bus tour in Savannah brought me to despair. Calling modest resorts and requesting a room with two beds—for my friend Connie and me—makes me focus sadly on loss, because there is no George on these vacations to cuddle with as we had in those great queen-sized beds. Times like these make me remember the huge king-sized bed that George and I once shared, laughing because we had to shout across the bed to talk. And there are the thousands of tiny day-to-day hurts that bring grief home to stab my heart.

Fortunately for me, some of my friends and my sister, Jo— all single for one reason or another—stayed by my side for comfort and friendship. Seven years later, Josephine herself would die and leave me once again without a best friend.

And, sadly, the widows in my life have increased their numbers; they are a source of joy and laughter and company. For most of our outings and trips, George would have elected to stay home with his dogs and sports, but the thought of him waiting at home would have been of endless comfort.

Sitting alone in the diner, I am drawn to a far booth, to the couple doting on the small child. They are the grandma and grandpa, and once more I am lost in the loss, in the realization that George will never have a catch with his grandsons Zack and Luke, or be entertained by our granddaughters Alyssa, Danielle, or Alexandra—the three little tintypes of his daughters—and tears well up, even now.

Grandparenting alone is acutely painful. I'm heartbroken when I see two older people together, obviously taking their little grandchildren to the ball game or the park. As I babysit on the long nights my kids are away or at the movies, there's no one to say, "Please George, see what little Zack wants," or, "Please George, get Danielle a drink of water," or "George, let the dog out while I feed Alexandra."

And, in the middle of the night, when those crazy thoughts that I sometimes have arise, there's no one to run them by—if George were there, he would calm my thoughts, and his voice of reason would save me. Often I ask myself, *What would George tell me about these foolish thoughts? How would he get me to see that this, too, shall pass?*

## Visiting My Closets

THE UNEXCEPTIONAL FRONT hall closet shares space with the small entrance foyer, welcoming visitors to our cozy home. It is so much more than that to me. It reflects the old life with George, with some new touches.

I still hang guests' coats in that refrigerated closet when the weather is mild; it is too cold there for wintertime hangings. If I must, I warn guests that I will remove their coats before they plan to leave, to warm them a bit. The little entrance hall doubles as an icebox for beer or soda when the kitchen one is too full at holiday time.

The never-repainted closet shows remnants of old blue and yellow paint, and as I open the door, it greets me unchanged. I ignore the two vacuum cleaners lodged right in front of me and run my hand over the satin of George's NY Giants jacket, which is bright blue and squashed to one side. Hanging next to the football coat is George's one lone sport jacket, which I have saved. Enthusiastically, I gave George's

Army field coat to my seventeen-year-old grandson, Zack. It's raggedy, but cool for teenagers to wear. Next, two more items I cannot seem to part with: George's button-down grey shirt and the old familiar plaid jacket, both of which I wear now and then. On to the closet in the den; it was always George's clothes closet—I got the one in the bedroom. His closet now holds all my office supplies: paper, envelopes, extra blankets, the metal box, and a great plastic tub cradling all the soulful Mass cards and messages of sympathy I received when George died. I rarely peek into that box; someday I'm sure I will.

My closet does not speak of anything special, except that surely I am a pack rat. I keep all the clothes, even the ones that do not fit, with high hopes. The two sentimental dresses are the bright blue worn to Chrissi and Mike's wedding, and the eggplant one worn to Claudy and Paul's wedding. Maybe I'll wear one to my nephew Michael's wedding soon.

Climbing the stairs to my daughters' room, I enter the great sunny raised attic they shared, now looking neatly like a preschool classroom; it includes a dollhouse, cradles, doll strollers, dress-up clothes, books, and a blackboard for the grandchildren when they visit. The girls' wardrobes, lovingly built by George, now hold some bits and pieces they've left behind, alongside bridesmaid dresses they no longer care about.

The next closet, another of George's projects, is one of the attic storage spaces the girls used to call the "Silent Scream" closet, as they compared it to one seen in a horror movie from their youth. Not scary any more, it is lighted and crammed: the girls' satin wedding gowns preserved in boxes and gossamer tissue paper; a big trunk filled with old costumes from their dancing school days, which are now excellent dress-ups for my granddaughters; a box containing school drawings and reports that the girls will find when I no longer live here; and more remnants of the life George and I lived together, way in the very back of the closet—his old fishing rods, his ancient golf clubs, a great fish tank where the hamsters once lived, and long slender pieces of wood that George "just might need for something someday." Those special treasures are untouched and silent for these many years; they take up little space and when I have the occasion to open that old door, the memories flood my consciousness and I am both glad and sad.

# 48

## Balancing My Life . . . 2009 and Beyond

I TURNED SEVENTY ON September 24, 2009 and, as I typed the words and they appeared on the starkly white page, huge droplets of tears fell upon the black computer keys. This silly, minor happening seems to have turned my world upside down. Ashamed of even mentioning the fact of my stupid birthday, I am sorry—sorry for making a "big deal" out of a birthday, when I have so much to be grateful for.

That day, as I had my nails painted, every thought that entered my head caused fat tears to roll down my cheeks. The thoughts came clearly—suddenly, I missed George more than I had in many years (it had been seventeen), and I felt really quite sorry for myself. *"Why do I have to be alone?"* George had been a voice of reason in my life and supported me even in my sometimes craziness. And then I thought of the tough things in life—and I cried some more.

There were three little kittens in my yard and I was feeding their mother. On my birthday, my neighbor and I were able to catch the kittens and put them in the basement. I wondered, *Are we doing a good thing? Is their mother sad? Wild to begin with, will they calm down? Will we find them homes?* It's foolishness, all foolishness, and I was unable to stop the dialogue. *How will I make it through all these questions?*

My mood seemed insurmountable, even as I apologized for all the nonsense, and recalled all the misery in the world. There is chaos in families all around me, and still I suffer the little things. There are homeless children I should be picturing, not homeless kittens. Our people have lost their jobs and their health care. My mind ran blazing forward: *What if this happens, what if that happens? How can I stop the chatter?* I know me—I'm rational, even, and utterly balanced. That day, I actually felt unbalanced and free falling into sadness.

As I wrote, I had no idea where my ramblings would take me. I hoped they would lead me to calmness, to peace, and to knowledge that the worst-case scenarios we often conjure up rarely happen. I hoped to feel gratitude to overtake the fears, so I could be happy in this lovely seventieth year—so I could feel gratitude for my health, for my loving family, for my adorable grandchildren, and for the rich days we spend together just living our lives. I'm searching for it, opening my heart to it, and just hoping for the overhanging clouds to open to allow the warming sun to enter.

If only I could stop the tears long enough to let the sunshine in.

The dawn of a beautiful new day found me better, as I dug out of my dark hole, small shovelful by small shovelful. Chores pulled me up, and the work of feeding the tiny, hungry kittens jolted me to wakefulness. My research on oral contraception in dogs and cats excites me, and I sent e-mails and made calls. Perhaps there is light at the end of my tunnel. I have been there before, when George was sick, and I used those exact words when I spoke at the party to celebrate my promotion at the Board of Education; "I have been in a dark, sad tunnel," I whispered into the microphone, and, as I drew my emotional speech to a close, "There is light at the end of my tunnel." Recalling these words, and knowing I would be happy again, I prettied myself, and drove off to have lunch with friends.

# 49

# Friends . . . Through the Years

E VELYN HAS BEEN IN my life since I was four years old. She was *just there* when I needed her. Never asking me to explain my decisions about George to her, she simply supported whatever I chose to do. I leaned heavily on her presence, and she helped me care for the animals in George's absence. Her presence in my life is a blessing I still treasure. She once paid George and me the ultimate compliment, saying that we were the ideal couple—until one day she heard one of our rip-roaring "disagreements," and thereafter had a more realistic view of our marriage. She knew George and I had a relationship that was special and sometimes volatile.

Janet and Ruben still miss George so; they were our closest couple friends, and now I am no longer a couple. They include me in their lives any way they can, spending early New Year's

Eves with me—always a difficult celebration. They make me laugh, and they never fail to tell a funny story about "what George would do or say," especially when they hear about some of the salaries doled out to baseball players—George would have been incredulous. "Nobody is worth those figures!" he would have screamed. We all agree that George would never have paid the price for a box at either the old *or* the new Yankee Stadium. He always claimed he preferred the upper decks, saying he could view the game better from up in the heights. Or even better, he'd rather plop in front of the TV at home or in the yard with the dogs by his side, with food that was "free" and more delicious. Janet and Ruben speak of George often, and remind me that he is never far from their thoughts—especially when they enter their "Mets Room." When Janet and Ruben planned to convert their attic space into a special refuge for Mets' fans—in blue, orange, and white, complete with posters, pictures, and all manner of Mets memorabilia—George had been on the spot to help them. The joke is—the way Janet and I tell the story—that we (Janet and I) helped build the Mets room; meanwhile, our only contribution was to supply the real workers—George and Ruben—some food now and then, and tell them, "Wow, looks great, guys!"

And then, of course, there are my neighbors Josephine and John. Even now when we see each other in the driveway, especially in spring or summer—or in winter, in the snow—there is a little shock that George is missing from the scene. I believe that George's illness and death has brought us closer together, as close as family. We need to be close; we need to cling to each other, so that the losses in life are not so painful.

Connie

Of course, my friend Ruth stayed with me during the first horrific weeks of George's illness. She had come from California for Chrissi and Mike's wedding, and stayed on to give me comfort and support. We went everywhere together during those first weeks, from the hospital meetings to the bank closing, and even to my office when I went back to work.

When Connie and I met on that day over thirty-five years ago when George and I moved into the house next door, I had no idea how our lives would intertwine, or how our friendship would grow into an iron bond, never to be broken.

I must thank my friend Connie for bringing me along on her journey and helping to open my heart and mind to women's issues. I was oblivious to so much that was going on in the world.

How was I to know that she would be my constant companion traveling through my grief with me, when George became sick some eighteen years later? My haunting recollection of that time is that whenever I called Connie to hold my hand, accompany me to lawyers, or see George in the hospital or nursing home, she never, *ever* had something else to do. She always, *always* had time for me and my grief, for the whole year George lay in his sleeping state and beyond, when the grief often took over my life—she was there.

All my friends let me do what I had to do without judgment.

## The Here and the Now

GEORGE IS LOOKING down on us, protecting us, being happy in heaven with the animals . . . we may say this, but I'm not so sure. What I am sure of is that sadness overwhelms me as I think of all George has missed.

When he was struck ill, we were reveling in our alone time in the empty nest, leaving pettiness behind. Enthusiastically, we insisted on our two weekends a year when—escaping from kids, animals, and cares—we felt renewed and refreshed. Those retreats are missing. Lost times with our grandchildren are particularly painful to contemplate. I'm angry that our five precious grandchildren will never know their Grandpa George, that I don't get to babysit with my husband.

Happily, George always had children in his life—our nieces and nephews, as well as great nieces and nephews. And then there was Daniela. Daniela, his little friend next door, born three years before George died, and with whom he was in love. He knew her intimately from the moment she was born, and she was so charming he could not resist loving her. Having such a relationship with Daniela was as close to having a grandchild as George would come. Each afternoon after work as I drove down my block toward our house, I could expect to see George standing outside with Daniela in his arms or by his side, eagerly waiting to report, "You should hear what she just said," or, "Theresa, just wait till you see how amazing she is with the dog!" He was completely smitten—wasn't it a joy that she came into his life?

Our young grandson Zachary George, now eighteen, slim and looking like a man with his long dark curly hair and hazel eyes, resembles George. He is inquisitive about his grandpa and it is bittersweet, painful, and joyful for me to tell him about George. Sadly, they will never catch a ball together or wrestle on the grass, watch a ballgame together or share their favorite musical greats. Neither will George ever thrill to the gorgeous freckled face of his little granddaughter Danielle Jo, or to his stunning, golden-haired granddaughter Alyssa Rose. And there is the tall and inquisitive Luke Robert to have fun with, and last but far from least—the impish image of her mother—Alexandra Nicole. Some resentment remains that George is not here for this most delicious part of our lives. And so we continue to talk about George, and never forget what he meant to our family—we tell the little anecdote about when Zack was only two, and we delighted

Danielle, Alex, and Willie

in how he could already swing that bat in a way that his Grandpa George would have been proud; Danielle Jo thrills me when she telephones to tell me that the Yankees are winning (or losing) and I daydream about how much George would have loved to share this special joy with her; and now the latest event that would be shared with George—twenty-five years since we sent our Christine off to college—we will all be saying goodbye to Chrissi's son, Zack, as he pursues his college dreams.

Life's joys live side by side with the fact that I miss George every day. I lament the leisurely trips we might have taken, perhaps cross-country; I ache at the pain of simply missing each other in the every day. What I find the most bittersweet of all is that I have lost the only person who loved and adored me when I was sixteen years old, who would have remembered me before wrinkles creased my eyes, and before walking long distances was a challenge—one who would have shared these past twenty years with me, these years rich and bursting

Zack, Alyssa, Luke

with life. This gift I have lost is great—the greatest. And then, we would have been there to take care of each other, for a while. It's dangerous to dwell on these thoughts, so I let in the gratitude for the happy times.

Delighted to have had him share my life for over thirty years, including the teenage years, I am a different woman from the one devastated so long ago when George died. I feel joyful because George continues to live in his daughters, who were the true loves of his life; he lives in his two sons-in-law, who came into his last years and for whom he had such high hopes; he truly lives in five magnificent grandchildren, whom he never knew, but who will know him through all of us. He continues to live when, upon an evening, we share his poetry with friends visiting our home, and they are inspired by his words, and come to know him a little. We read his poems and think of him; we bring him close to us each Christmas when someone in our circle writes "The Christmas Letter"—a letter to George in which we tell him all that is going on in our family

We carry on joyously

It's Thanksgiving and the fun times roll on

or in the world, or in which we just tell him we remember him and are thinking of him, so that his memory will go on keeping us company, keeping us safe, and keeping him in our hearts.

Amazingly, almost twenty years are gone, and so much has happened in life—a life George has not shared for a long time. Perhaps that's why I hang on to some of the past by politely refusing to think of selling the home we bought together. There, I can look around at George's collection of sports books and movie trivia; I can gaze at the print of Joe DiMaggio with his mighty swing staring back at me. I cuddle with only a furry gray cat in our bedroom, where I sleep on George's side of the bed. I gaze out at the little wooden tables he built, now crumbling in the backyard, but from which I cannot part.

And I have had dozens of dreams—dreams about George and about Ray, too—which seemed so very real to me. Just for a bit of levity, the other night I had a vivid dream of George, and—guess what?—I had given him my book to read. He was reading it and glancing away, reading and glancing away. I said, "Why aren't you reading?" His answer? "Well, it's kind of boring." I was horrified, and when I awoke, I said a little prayer that this was not so!

Yet it seems as if, little by little, parts of George are disappearing, mementos are crumbling and memories are fading. That's why I've written this memoir; in refusing to allow him to disappear, all of my readers have gotten to know George— just a little—and the loss is lessened.

# 50

## Christmas . . . December 2012

GLIDING TOWARD THE final chapters of my memoir, I became aware of how far I have come from that first Christmas, and George, and the silver thread. I have taken pleasure in so many days since then and see that fun and humor have found me again. In December 2011, I had written the following:

*I first glimpsed those damn sparkling white lights in a window a few weeks ago, and I thought to myself, "And it's not even Thanksgiving!"'*

*I told myself,* Don't panic; there's time.

*Suddenly it was December . . . the 4th . . . the 5th. Okay, I decided to begin early—still, I didn't panic.*

*All year long, Christmas boxes have stared at me from the basement and from the attic—I had pushed them from my consciousness.*

*Suddenly, slight panic began to creep in, but the Christmas music softened my mood. I trekked up and trekked down, bringing up and bringing down small bins—I could not carry the big ones.*

*Outside lights were a challenge; I had to give up on hanging glittering icicles high up on the peaks of the roof. I settled for a spotlight, illuminating the antique Santa and a pretty wreath with a red bow. Last year, I had succumbed to purchasing a weatherproofed, shiny, lighted tree to dazzle the front lawn— and damn, now only half the lights worked. I tossed it. I purchased new illumination for the fence and electrified radiant red "presents" for the stoop. Outdoor-strength extension cords, indoor surge protectors for the tree and the miniature lighted village were needed, with cash flying out.*

*I placed the little individualized houses on the desk, making sure each little window glowed as I hooked each one to the other in an intricate dance.*

*As usual, serious cursing—too wicked to repeat—ensued, as I blamed George for being dead. Christmas house decorations were* his *job. My memories made it seem like yesterday—I could see him spending hours in the basement as he tested each and every bulb on the long strings of lights to save them. I hated that useless task, so once again—in just a few seconds—I tossed anything that did not work.*

*Then there was the Christmas tree stand. Last year, my daughter Claudine had come to assist me in placing the living tree, always almost six feet tall, into the stand. The stand was corroded and rusted, and the bolts had refused to move. Claudy rushed to Garden World to buy a new one; she admitted to choosing the most expensive one, not knowing its outrageous* cost until she was at the checkout counter. She wouldn't tell me how much she paid for it, but I laughingly told her it would be willed to her when I die. This year I found the new stand shiny and ready to go. Treasured holiday towels, given to me by my good friend Ruth, were lovingly hung in the bathroom, and bright red tablecloths were ready for the big night, Christmas Eve, which I host every year.

Soon enough, I attended the spirited chorus presentations of two of my granddaughters and they cheered me. The kids helped me decorate the tree after I endured another stressful trip to Garden World to choose one that was fat, but not too tall, with a trunk that would fit the new stand.

As Christmas Eve approached, I was almost ready—maybe one more trip to Toys R Us or Kohl's for a last minute gift—and in the next day or two it would be off to my local fish market for the traditional shrimp and mussels, and other savory ingredients for the Christmas Eve feast.

Some moments, I want to be done with all the upheaval and activity, but I won't give in to the temptation to pull back—not yet. On some future Christmas when I choose a small artificial tree and pull it out of a box fully lighted, I will know I'm done— I'll know I've truly become my mother's daughter, and that will be fine with me.

### A Season For Hope

The holiday season is coming near
With good hope and kindly cheer,

We give and get gifts of worth
To celebrate our Savior's birth.

We feast and toast 'til body's filled
And then sit back with conquered will;

But not I, for all I know,
For warmth and comfort is not always so—

There's a need for all to share a dream,
For helpless creatures to live serene;

Their plight is dark with hunger reached,
They suffer so, 'til death brings peace.

Their only hope is in man's grace,
That he will help them find their place.
So when you think of noel glee,
Let's remember what should really be.

It's hope for *all* life for us to shout,
'Cause that's what Christmas is all about.

~A Special Poem by George

# 51

## Yet Another Ending . . . July 2012

T IS THE DAY BEFORE the end. When I awake tomorrow morning, I will wait for the crew to arrive to begin the demolition of the wooden deck that has served as our patio and retreat for the past twenty-five years. The planked structure with its side railings and decorative door was lovingly built by George and our friend Ruben. I am filling with tears as I contemplate yet another ending.

Gone are the days when the wood was smooth and shiny. Now it is splintered, with uneven dangerous pitted planks and missing bolts—utter disrepair. I know it is time for it to go, but still, I cannot stop the sobbing. I hope I can get all the tears out now, so I will be stoic and without reddened eyes tomorrow morning when the men arrive to pull it apart, and install a new, easier-to-care-for cement patio.

Our deck was the site of hundreds of yummy barbecues with friends and family featuring George's special burgers, which were laced with onions, juicy, and topped with cheese. Even coworkers from my office invited to lunch on the tasty morsels were duly impressed with George's wit and culinary talent.

Then there were the thousands of evenings when George sat outside late into the night—after I had fled the torturous mosquitoes—watching his beloved Yankees, his dogs by his side, his sunflower seeds in his lap. This deck most probably provided various stray cats and kittens shelter from rain and snow in past years. This fact is chilling for me to contemplate, and I hope future strays will find shelter in my garage—left with one square purposely punched out so they can easily enter.

Josephine next door reminds me how bittersweet the sight of the deck devastation will be for her, too, as she recalls her first days in her new home when she met George and saw him building this veranda—he was so proud of it. Later, after George died, the deck continued to give us pleasure as it held the kiddie pool and the sand-and-water table so enjoyed by our grandchildren.

In recent years, the beautiful old redwood picnic table with matching picnic benches was replaced by a sleek glass-and-metal table and chairs. The old-fashioned real redwood set had two-inch-thick planks and was sturdy—just like George. We didn't get rid of it entirely; it rests under the new deck in Claudine and Paul's backyard, cradling various back-yard supplies and toys. As I notice it from time to time, it is a sweet reminder of George.

Well, here I sit, waiting for the deck's end to come. I can't stop crying, and I will finish my piece tomorrow after the deed is done. Right now I am dreading the morning to come. I need to call a friend; I need to cry with someone.

Morning has come and I am still here, and still teary as I chat with the young men who will do the work. They probably think I am crazy, and so I am, a little. I am already thinking of ways I can make the plain cement patio look more cozy: put a pretty wood fence somewhere on the side, add an "I don't know what."

How about a dozen bagels for the workers now, and to cheer me up?

And the next day—the cement is done—it looks nice. With a lump in my throat, I offer my own personal ending. George's initials, "GC," will forever grace my new cement in a little corner—with no one the wiser, just we, his family, to admire and remember.

# 52

## And What About My Parents?

### My Mother, Rose

Dear Mom,

I visited your grave the other day—Bob and I had fun. Brother and baby sister walking, talking, reminiscing, and enjoying the sunny day. I rarely visit, but I see you in other, significant ways.

You and I had taken the bus, lunch in a brown paper bag, to another cemetery long ago; I was four. You made it fun and a game—a picnic. No fear of cemeteries. Thanks. And so I think of you.

We rode all manner of New York City buses and subway trains—the C and the R and the L—to visit relatives in strange and faraway boroughs. I came to know all my extended family—all the cousins, aunts, and uncles. I learned to care for others as you did, and so no fear of traveling far and wide. Thanks. And so I think of you.

I babysit my grandchildren as you did yours—always giving. I learned to give. No fear of relationships. Thanks. And so I think of you.

Then you were sick and sometimes didn't know us. But you always told me, "Your hair looks so pretty." I learned to compliment others. Thanks. And so I think of you.

You passed no guilt on to me. "You don't have to come," you'd say. And sometimes I didn't come. I learned not to pass on guilt. Thanks. And so I think of you.

With love and gratitude,
Your daughter, Theresa

## My Father, Rocco

Dear Dad,

Some years ago, I wrote a message in a card and mailed it to you, for no specific purpose. No birthday or occasion; I just wanted to tell you that "I would not be the person I am today without your guidance and example."

The variety of books always on your night table encouraged me to be a reader and thus a writer.

You encouraged me—to take the "Commercial Course" in high school; not the absolute best advice, but I took this advice and it led me to the joys of a most rewarding career as a secretary and executive assistant. I never regretted this path, and again, it has made me who I am. You traveled without fear—and so I am a fearless traveler.

My dear Jo, and our Dad, Rocco

You gave me freedom—even at a young age—and you expected me to make good decisions, only admonishing me, "Don't take any 'funny cigarettes' from anyone."

You were kind and smiled often—so tender to your little old Italian mama and your old *zio,* Pepe (Uncle Joe, who lived to be ninety-nine)—such simple traits, yet they conveyed important lessons of caring for those around me, looking for the good, and feeling empathy for those less fortunate, especially the animals.

Just a small sampling of all you were to me. And as I said to Mom—*Thanks.*

(as you always signed your cards)
Your "ever-loving"
Theresa

273

# Thanks for the Memories

AVING WATCHED TELEVISED coverage of the touching funeral service for Teddy Kennedy, I was moved to write my own page of gratitude to share during a special family celebration honoring my 70th birthday and the 80th birthday of my brother, Bob. As none of us are ever around for our own funerals, I decided to write about my gratitude for that fitting occasion.

*I'm so pleased to share my 70th birthday celebration with that of my beloved older brother, Bob, whose most special 80th birthday is soon to come, on February 22, 2010. My brother has been and continues to be my mentor and friend—but that is another long and inspiring story.*

*Saddened that our beautiful middle sibling, Josephine, is not here to help us celebrate, we are thankful to feel her spirit in this room through her precious daughters, Diane and Carol, and in her wonderful grandchildren, Michael (and his Tracy), Jillian, Natalie, Peter, and Joseph. And I am always grateful to have my dearest nieces, who have been—since my thirteenth birthday—*

Our family celebrated!

*my first babies, and who are now my friends and confidants, all women I am proud of. At the tender age of thirteen, my heart filled when "my" first girl, Paula, was born. I was overcome with love for her . . . I didn't know I was practicing for the births of all my nieces: Diane, Valerie, Carol, and Gail—and for my great nieces and nephews—and of course, ultimately, for my own wonderful daughters, Christine and Claudine. My gratitude to my Christine for never forgetting George's and my anniversary through the years; and to Claudine, who helped me transition from my role as George's wife to a woman on my own, as we designed her wedding dress, searched for houses, shopped, and just had fun; and for the sons they have brought into my life—they help me care for my home and my life. Mike is a much-loved doctor to family, friends, and me; and Paul generously plants my stunning spring flower garden each year.*

*My girls and their families have brought joy to my life—and what greater gift could they have given? Then—for me the most delightful of all—the next generation: Bobby and his granddaughter, Courtney; Jo's grandchildren; and my own glorious grandchildren, Zack, Alyssa, Danielle, Luke, and Alexandra.*

*Once more, thanks for the memories . . . the vacations, the picnics, the special occasions such as our trips on the railroad to Manhattan . . . the Christmases and holidays, the stories and the sleepovers. I hope you took pleasure in the stories of my life. They are all about me, and about George and me—George, my beloved husband, gone these many years, but still so much a part of all of us—and it's about all of you.*

*I am blessed to have had as special a friend as Evelyn has been to me—for sixty-five years—and in case I forget to say it, thank you* all, *from my heart, for being my family, and for the great party.*

*And now a sweet postscript: How fortunate I am now to have to delight my days and gather into my family Jillian and Ben's precious twins, Juliana and Scarlet, my great, great nieces.*

*With love, from Theresa, Mom, "Auntie," Grammy, Mimi*

# Epilogue

THE IDEA OF WRITING this story about George has defined my life. For the past twenty years the memories have been alternately swirling and dancing below the surface of my conscious thoughts—eventually, they found their way to the pages of my memoir. In the early days my work consisted of reading about death and dying and investigating these phenomena. I became less frightened and more comforted than in the past, spurred on to continue writing fearlessly.

I never cease wondering, *Is George with us, seeing all, watching over us?* Who can say? When he was struck down but still with us, we came to believe he was attached to us by a silver thread—half in this world and half in the other.

Unfortunately, it took George's death to make the narrative of this book happen—and fortunately, his story and mine gave me a voice I might never have known I had. That voice im-mortalized George. If he had not been attached by the silver thread and had his passing not been so curious—and if I had not been moved to write about him—his death, although sad, would have been just one of many heartbreaking but un-written widow's stories.

No longer attached by that silver thread, he travels with me on my daily journey, defining me, as I work to see these words in print for all to see, know, and celebrate.

During that painful year and forever after, the words on George's tombstone and in the song—*Turn on your heart light*—echo for me: *Turn on your heart light—I'll be right here.*

We are here for each other!

# About the Author

Theresa Cerrigone, "Terri," lives in Flushing, New York with four cats and a few regular strays who gather at the garage; she feeds them each and every morning and night. This gathering of stray cats—who have all been spayed or neutered at Terri's expense—has taken place at the garage for the past forty years, a ritual established all those years ago by Terri's husband, George. A lover of animals, Terri dreams of the day she can once more invite a dog—an older one, like Terri herself—to share her life.

Terri attends memoir-writing workshops regularly and revels in the company of growing grandchildren and a close circle of friends. She is contemplating her upcoming trip to Alaska, and she is in the midst of her goal of completing individual trips with each of her grandchildren. Terri and Zack visited Ruth in California when Zack was just fifteen, exploring exciting Tinseltown together. Terri took Alyssa and Danielle (then fourteen and twelve) on a fantastic train trip to Niagara Falls. She is currently planning an exciting trip with Luke—at ten going on eleven, he is eager to travel to exotic places. And of course, when nine-year-old granddaughter Alexandra is a little older, it will be her turn to take a memorable journey with her grandmother. Terri is not contemplating moving from the beloved home she shared with George any time soon.

At seventy-three, Terri feels that her life is good. She is planning her next book, which will be about the pets that Terri has known, and the importance of spaying and neutering both dogs and cats, and the protection of all our four-legged furry friends.

Terri's e-mail address is reddogg2426@nyc.rr.com.

CPSIA information can be obtained at www.ICGtesting.com
Printed in the USA
BVOW10s0714300813

329926BV00008B/10/P

9 780989 399970